Cameroon Anthology of Poetry

T0319202

Bole Butake

Langaa Research & Publishing CIG
Mankon, Bamenda

Publisher:
Langaa RPCIG
Langaa Research & Publishing Common Initiative Group
P.O. Box 902 Mankon
Bamenda
North West Region
Cameroon
Langaagrp@gmail.com
www.langaa-rpcig.net

Distributed in and outside N. America by African Books Collective
orders@africanbookscollective.com
www.africanbookcollective.com

ISBN: 9956-790-00-1

DISCLAIMER
All views expressed in this publication are those of the author and do not
necessarily reflect the views of Langaa RPCIG.

Table of Contents

I

CAMEROON

Margaret Afuh

To Countryside

1. Mother of nature sitting still,
   Counting your treasures from nature's mill
   Endlessly all day long you perform your duty.
   Countryside, enchantress, a paragon of beauty.

2. Roaring streams betwixt rolling hills,
   Endless plains all calm and still,
   But for the swaying scattered trees,
   Dancing to the tune of the gentle breeze.

3. Grazing herds on the dark green flanks,
   Fluttering wings from the winding banks,
   High and low in the cold morning grey,
   The kingfisher fishes its prey.

4. Though far from his kind a lone traveller,
   Round him sweet happy friends, quiet crawlers,
   The singing wind in the thick, green foliage;
   The waving plants from the dark – brown tillage.

5. Gliding birds and dazzling cascades like fountains,
   Spray down the old, giant rugged mountains
   A blooming meadow blue meekly lies,
   A humming honey bee round the flowers flies.

6. A purer and cooler air ne'er was found
   For who'er by sorrow or sadness is bound;
   An atmostphere serene and inspiring,
   For the altar and who'er to the pen is aspiring.

7. Sweet nature, pure as morning rose,
   Pain-healing balm, gentle dove
   Dictator of many an immortal verse,

Generator of virtues diverse.

8. Countryside, from creation, the springboard
   From which grew civilisation
   To everlasting thou art the mainstay of life,
   Nourishing man like a good wife.

March 3rd, 1986, Kumba

My Mother

1. When in my life there is sadness,
   When in my life there is sunshine,
   At every phase of my temperament,
   In every drop of my blood,
   There is this dear figure,
   Who is my mainstay and my all.

2. Between towering gigantic trees,
   Shading a clearing large.
   From which a serpentine smoke
   Rockets into the blue sky.
   She, bent with a cutlass and a hoe,
   Cuts and digs in toil and sweat;
   She tills, and plants and reaps for me.

3. Once she would sit and sew on her machine,
   At her window from rise to set,
   Or sit in a hut behind bottles of palm wine;
   To sell and fetch some coins home;
   To sit there all day long, watching and calling,
   Tis crippling for time moves on crutches;
   Yet, she does it all for me.

4. When I lie writhing in agony,
   When I toss and twist about in pain,
   When I am near the frontiers of this world,
   She runs far and wide to get herb and counsel;

Though dreadful her way, and death on her heel,
She wades her way through until I am restored.

5.   As I sit on this lonely day,
     Faced with the trials and controversies of this life,
     I think of your invulnerable love,
     And crave with an inextinguishable passion,
     To share with you always,
     My love, my wealth, my all,
     O my mother.
                              April, 1982, Yaounde

The Drunkard

1.   Behold him alone on the road.
     The knock-kneed, staggering drunkard,
     Howling his head out in mournful tunes.
     The peals of his singing ending in a crescendo,
     Re-echoing through the still moonlit night.

2.   The drunkard stumbles on head bent,
     Straining his eyes the dancing road to see,
     On his way home to his waiting wives,
     His arm firmly closing his raffia bag
     Containing his drinking horn and careless coins.

3.   "Ho! would someone open the door for me?"
     A sleepy owl coos and flutters into the shadow.
     "Would some woman show me the way?"
     A creaking sound from all six doors;
     Six hurricane lamps flush the way with light,
     And the drunkard staggers home.

                              1990, Limbe

Nol Alembong

The Hamadryad

Only drugged minds
saw any liniment
in the venomous spittle
emitted each minute
of the coiling seasons
spent in the barbed-wire fence
that spelled the triangular boundaries
of the neonate empire where the
hamadryad reigned in awful command.
Maybe they didn't notice that
after each majestic hiss walls of frogs
were bugged to what the wolf's lust for flesh.
Didn't they see they surgeons tupping
diseased bodies on wonky tables?
Didn't they see piercing tentacles spreading
on rose beds to harvest white petals?
Didn't they see the blind teaching
Sharp eyes how to read the hamadryad's bible?
And still, some mortgaged the air we breathe
for a mosaic of fragile fragments;
and our skinny trunks rolled with that of
the fat and greasy whale-like hamadryad
through twenty-five murky and stony ways.
And didn't the tortoise unveil
the dogmatics pf hamadryadism?
Weren't the halleluja cantors lined up
and made to stare at the mid-day sun
with their naked eyes?
But who will now tell me whether
hamadryadism breeds lambs?

Some Day For Sure

Oh, how snake-like the trembling cry
Twines the small of my brains!
The feeble cords of the voice
Spell the agonies of the Tortoise
Down trodden by the Elephant
But for how long will this last
When the tortoise's shell is hard to crack?
The journey may be too long and hard,
But was the chameleon not the first
To drum the long awaited message of death?
Where was Dog that thought
The race was his?

Exchanging Planes in Mid-Air

(To the memory of Okot p'Bitek)

I

The mother
Who they say
Is my small aunt,
The sister of my mother,
Calls me pagan.
She calls me the uncircumcised
As if she didn't eat palmoil
At the ritual when my manhood
Was exposed to elders and age mates alike
And its foreskin cut off
To let blood wet the earth
The blood
That quenched the thirst of our ancestors.

She says
Big hook has
Ruined me like faggots
That have been ruined by black ants.

She says
I don't go to church,
The whiteman's house of worship,
Because my books teach me
Strange things,
Things that make me
Turn my back to the god
Who they say lives in the sky.
Things that made me
Follow the black path
That leads to satan's chiefdom,
Things that shall make me
Feast in fires
In the country of wizards.
When I try to picture this mother of mine –
This black skin with white blood –
Sleep finishes in my head.

II

My mother
Who they say
Is my small sister
Is now the white god's child –
The white god who lives
In a country in the sky.
And she says
I am the child of the black god.
The black god
Who lives in rocks
And in streams
And in baobab trees.
She says
Her god is the true god.
That my god,
The god of my fathers
And my fathers' fathers,
Is a thing of the imagination.
But when all children
Had lice in their heads,

All at one time time.
This mother
Who they say
Is my mother's sister
Said I shouldn't
Clean their heads
All in one day
Because when it comes
To falling sick
They all will fall sick
In one-day –
All at once!
She said
I should clean
Nkeng's head today
Awung's head tomorrow
And Leke's head
The other tomorrow;
All this
Because when it comes
To falling sick
They all shouldn't fall sick
In one day.
But
This mother
Who is my mother's sister
Is the white god's child.
So,
When I think about
This cleaning of heads
On three different days
Sleep finishes in my head.

III

The mother
Who is my mother's sister
Worships her white god
On different days
Of the week.

This week, it is on *asieh*
And she joins the others
In the house of their white god
To shout like a male goat
Whose testicles are being removed.
They shout and stiffen their bodies
As if they have been attacked by tetanus.
They say
They are shouting praises to their god:
One would think their god is deaf,
One would think their god is an iguana.
Next week
They meet on *alung*
And shout as if they had
Never shouted before.
And the other week
They meet on *ankoah*
Not only to shout but to cry
As if their god has lost his brother.
When I asked her,
This woman who is my mother's sister.
Whether they have no fixed day
To worship their god
She said
The day was "sabat",
That it was number seven day
Of our eight-day week,
The day their white god
Chose to rest.
As if he had been
Splitting fire-wood
For six days running.
But,
When I think about this "sabat"
That has no fixed day in the week –
This week
It falls on *asieh*
Next week
It falls on *alung*
The other week

11

It falls on *ankoah* –
For true,
When I think about
This "Sabat"
That falls on
Different days
Of the week
Sleep finishes
In my head.

IV

The mother
Who is my mother's sister
Says strange things to me.
She quarrels with me
For sending my woman
To rest with her parents
When ever she had a stomach.
She says
My writing books
Is no excuse to stay alone
Especially when my woman
Is carrying a stomach.
She says
If you don't
Sleep with your woman
Now that she has a stomach
How will milk enter her breast?
But
When I try to imagine
What sleeping with a woman
Who has a stomach
Has to do with
The milk in her breast
Sleep finishes in my head.

Alobwed'Epie (1945-)

No Past, No Present, No Future

Africa south of the Sahara,
Only in verse her glorious past,
In reality, a haunting emptiness,
Not a word in print nor a stone upon a stone
But decaying thatch and mouldering wood
Plaguing my pride with endless questions.

Did those heroes in song live,
Did they dwell, did they reason,
Did they make war, did they scan the skies,
Was there a Pharaoh or a Confucius?
Look round and turn to evidence,
No, there is none, there's no evidence.

To know the past, scan the now,
And ask of a Washington or a Churchill,
And if there's none, hail him by name,
If there's none, seal your lips with a magic band,
For, cough, and the beasts of Maidanek (Nyerere apart)
Will draw their swords and slaughter,
And drag your bones on the old sands of fate.

As of now, was of old,
The vampire empires south of the Sahara,
Slug in moral crises, radiating –
Social, economic and political crisis.
What caused that, but saliva turned hemlock?
The worms go for the buds,
And so, posterity destroy.

The future is bleak,
There is melancholy,
As modern blowpipes gird their loins,
Ready to spew red rain upon the land

Once liberated, now plundered
By patriots turned traitors.

So, restrain your borrowed code in song
In chastising and castrating the lender
For, the evils that men do live long after them,
These evils are theirs and ours only;
From patron to matron, of past and present.

The Election Day

Tat, tat, tat, tat a tat tatatata,
The African electorate spew their ballots.
Tat, tat, tum, tum, tat tatata, tum, tum, tum,
Puffy faces peer through bunker holes
Beholding ghettos crumble under blast,
Tum, tum, tum, tumtumtumtumtum,
While panicky skeletons stampede,
Littering cratered streets with bleached bodies.
Tum, tat, tat, tat, tum, tum, tumtumtum, tatata,
The temporarily spared, clamour in vain,
Tum, tatatat tum, tumtumtum, tatata, tat,
Spilling over unknown borders.
Outcasts of the earth, wandering in the void,
Tasting the nauseous broth of Ethiopia
In gruesome march to eternity.
Tum, tum tum, tatatat, tat, tum, tat,
The world starts in awe, but helpless,
For this is surely an internal affair,
Tat, tum, tum, tum, tat, tat, tatata,
And only the solid red lead emitting muzzle
Can conduct the elections free and fair.
Tat, tum, tat, tum, tat, tum, tum ,tum, tum,
From the carnage emerge the elected
Skulls of hornbills empty;
Wielding tanks, bombs and Bayonets,
For brains, charisma and fortitude.
Shame Africa.

The Monument

The Emperor built a monument
In his image and glory,
And gilded it from toe to crest,
And at its feet we laid palm fronds.

Guards stood watch by day and night,
In sunshine and rain alike,
And it, in a circle backed,
To face the external foe.
On each nativity, 'sages' the world over,
Paid homage to emperor and monument,
And the world went round in glory,
For the animate and the inanimate.

Then after three scores the Emperor,
In the way of all flesh went,
And the circle of guards turned inward,
And with raised guns faced the enemy.

With a click the boom went up
And a mighty cloud of dust rose,
And where the monument and some
Die-heart guards stood,
Lo! An empty space became.

Beware then of monuments self-erected,
Be they in print or in stone,
For only posterity real monuments erects,
And those, for eternity last.

Gregory Achu Ashi

The Spineless Heir

The first cock's impatience
Is now eroded
And it is he must
Signal moon's blossoming ripeness
And hence the spineless
Women's home-coming.

The foreboding is heart-rending
For thorny weeds have sprouted
On the war-tested, time-honoured
Roof of the valorous;
Mushroom-wise, they
Have thus sprouted!

What rendering will I give
In the world of broad spears
And shields of steel
That my name is War?
But I have anointed palm-fronds
For an heir.

Death you have hallowed
In the guise of wine
But yours won't be
A death like mine.
I have never tased of death,
For death's off-spring
Is none but me!

A forest of hair
Your head has now become;
Ad your reward
A week's mourning declared
For a tiger's given birth

To a slimy shrew-mouse.

Were you wood in the
Thick, thick bushes
Women would fetch
With their bare, matchetless hands
For the male tool
Would be too virile for you
Who should now mourn who?

A Dream

The dream dragged on;
Death was the key-note:
A corpse became the
Meat for the funeral
Yet it was his own corpse!

How it had happened
Only Meyigi, the Great
Holds the knot.
But the mourners and dancers
Mourned and sang;
And then the corpse
Joined in the dirge.

And they all sang:
"The funeral goat
Which descends with the corpse
In to the grave
Is the corpse's own son!"

The dirge continued:
"Our main dancer's eyes
Are cloudy;
Mother hare crossed the brok
With ears backwards stretched;
Off-spring hare has no option
Repent, you both

Or risk our bilious wrath."

As they sang
The corpse went down –
Went down hesitantly
As if in protest.
And he panted, grunted, sweated
To lower his own corpse
Into his own grave.

As the black clay earth,
His own colour,
Began its journey
Down the yawning grave,
He started, gaped, stared;
But this time in his bed,
Bamboo hard.

All had vanished:
Mourners and corpse.
What had happened
He now knew not.

The sun's smile in the East
Was getting broader and broader
All had vanish'd
Into nothingness;
Yet one truth haunted him:
He had taken part in
His own burial.

Ben Besingi

At the Grave-Yard

Here in death kingdom
Silence reigns over the dead;
And everyone in his house of tomb,
In his own prison of liberty,
In silence reigns.

How deep and lonely they sleep!
And how long will they sleep
In these pits so steep and deep?
They all lie besieged.

Here they lie, cold,
Blind, silent, motionless, thoughtless,
In this obscure and dreadful place
Where all the roads of life converge;
Where the rich and the poor,
The strong and the weak, and the great
Have all been levelled to the ground.

As in some traditional celebration,
The eucalyptus trees sway and dance in the air,
Their needle leaves sighing in the wind,
While sparrows fly around
Chirp, chirping aloud
As if in mockery of man
At his failure for eternal rule.

The Countryside in May

February is a poor nurse and provider:
The whole countryside is suffering from famine,
And the harmattan-and-sun bleached hillsides
Are pale-brown and sullen.

But when May comes,
Like a good and devoted mother
She spreads a thick blanket of clouds in the sky
While the vegetation suckles the nipples of the rain.

Like a Princess in a green flower dress
Just finished making up for a wedding banquet,
The entire countryside is glowing with life
Under the clear, calm May sky.

Bate Besong

The Beauty of Exile

Do not say you are abandoned
And deserted Friend
For it is the Beauty of your exile
That has shown how ugly we have become

Heroes have made their way
Along the Tcholliré swamps into nameless
Catacombs, martyrs:
Their limbs became too frozen
For them to rise to their feet, to walk

Observe now how these same jokers
Despoil the communal treasures
They brush with hasty steps the torture-chambers
Away;
To the zombie clamour of moronic processions.

Or, soon when these same revellers
Start running round again in circles
Then, the stench of alien obloquies, frothing
Ceaselessly

From a long-rutted
Ideology – very well –
Where are the hired runners
Who will bridge the firepower
Of our anger across the Mungo

If some limbs are still too weak
To stand on their feet, if, some brains
Are still too plaited with steel –
Gray streams?

Who will convert the broodings

Of these people over the past
Into bouquets to a new dawn?

So do not say you are abandoned
And deserted friend
It is the beauty of your exile
That has shown how ugly we have become.

The Grain of Bobe Augustine Ngom Jua

(For Sam Nuvalla Fonkem , Ngwa-Nyambodi & all...)

When Bobe Augustine Ngom Jua died
As leaves fell on the garden between
The slow chimes of the funerary bell, so gently-
The iguanas
Of our Cameroon history books

Who were left behind
Emerged from their prehistoric slime:
A sphinx of evil magic hung above my head
As they
Tore apart limb by limb
The primeval psaltery over the pine trees
Crying Bobe's fame.

He left behind
In those days, *(there was sadness
In your cheeks)* – all that time!
The grain to you who plough the prairies
Dread;
The droughts of the pharaohnic iguanas tearing
The barrages of the Nile

In the sad lonely hours long
We explored the reddened rubble
Of the sickle
For our farmers trapped in the renegade's plantation
Ah such hopeless nights hearts straining long

A voice grew hoarse.
Drop.
A decade gone.

And indeed these are no empty words
For if I have denuded fear
In your eyes again
It is so; here we are lacerating
This Earth with wounds
Inflicted to the tunes of the subtle
Gallows;
Of our own cultivation!
So you see?
(the plague on hour heads
if we fail the generation of young Dante)

For
We have too long applauded:
The pharaohs
Worming their ways back into their immense
Sphinxes of steel...

Envoi:
Ah! the time has come, Friend
To return from the mountain;
Shore the cavalier floods
Of the immortal Mungo

Or we shall find again tomorrow
In the garden
As dewfall spreads magic
Over the chameleon tongue
Of the iguana's perennial comeback

We shall find again once more
Bobe's seed, gone;
With the drought

If you don't remember this Friend
How shall the provincial grain sprout

25

And grow?

Bole Butake

My Woman Is a Tiger

My woman
She is a tiger.

Have you seen my woman
Or heard the mother of my house?
She was tall
As tall as the bamboo from Nsai bush;
Her skin as smooth as the grinding stone
As clear as the sand from Kifiang.
Her face round and smooth
And a mouth most ravishing had she.
Her eyes were as sparkling as hail-stones
And when she looked at you
The sting was equally soothing.

My woman
She was an otter.

The watermaid that honours none
But the worshipper
The servant at her footstool,
The priest at her shrine.

I was her servant for many moons;
I was the priest at her shrine
For many market days.

I worshipped and cursed
The moment I leapt into the light.
I pined and wept
The moment I saw the dark.

Would she never hear my prayer
Would she never hear my call

Would she never notice my slavery
Did she only see my fake contempt?

Oh! I wished I would/live   /not
I would drink but to remember.
All the moons of beautiful shapes and shades
Were drowned by this lonely star;
And people wondered.

My woman
She was a tiger.

The harmattan fire that consumed Bia
In a battle of wits with Wanti
His hunting peer.
The water that swept away
The season's entire corn harvest
And Nkasai took the rope.
The disease that killed
The entire hen population
And there was none left for sacrifice.

My woman
She was

The fire that consumed me
Leaving nothing but cold, impotent ash.
The river that swept me away
Leaving nothing but withered stalks.
The disease that killed me
Leaving nothing but a worthless shell.

And now that I am ash
Now that I am impotent ash
Now that I am cold, impotent ash;
My woman is a tiger:
Madam Tortoise.

Restrictions

Once I walked down a village path
To the village stream.
It was the period of
The splitting of the sun
So that I had wet feet
By the time I got to the bank.
And, as there I stood,
There was a sudden rushing
From upstream; and the clear water
Of the stream
Turned brown as I watched.

Then I heard that ringing laugh,
I heard that voice so sweet and mellow,
And I knew what had pulled me
So early in the morning to the stream.
There she stood across the bank
Chattering with her brothers and sisters.
They had come to fetch water
For each of them had a waterpot.
And now the water had turned brown
(There must me a storm upstream)
And there I stood ignored and abandoned.

I had heard that ringing laugh
Sail up to my ears as I sat
In my hut on the side of the hill
Where I had lost my only cow.
It had become too wild for milking
And I had paid a huntsman
To shoot it dead.
Now, as I lived in seclusion
Haunted by the spirit of my cow,
I often heard this ringing laugh,
This sweet voice, pulling softly
The chords that linked my body to soul.

And as I walked down the hill this morning
I felt like a carefree urchin
Going out on some new exploit.
But when again I heard that melody
As on the bank I stood
Scandalised by the sudden transformation
Of clear stream into dirtful water,
I knew that long I would wait
To be able to drink at the source.

Lament of a Warrior

What is the wailing for?
They have broken my back,
And seized my red feather;
The feather that was my pride.
Now my enemies can show their teeth
For they are pleased with my disgrace.
Now I am naked and helpless
For the feather that was my
Support is no more.
How I would beat my chest
And they would recoil in terror!
Who dared to show their faces
When the leopard roared?
Now they lie about in the market place
And talk in loud voices;
When before they would sneak off
With their tails between their legs.
Yes, they can now beat their chests
And declare 'Poison did the trick'.
All because of woman.

Emmanuel Fru Doh

Bamenda Chop Fire

Bamenda *chop fire*:
Camouflaged outfit
with guns in war-like readiness
hungry mouths perched on walkie-talkies
microphones gingerly gripped by crooks,
loaded jeeps zooming to and fro
transporting worn-out riot helmets.
In a trance they appear to be,
confused whether they swore
to eliminate or protect citizens
Bamenda *chop fire*.

Bamenda *chop fire*:
Babies, mothers, husbands,
Women: girls, the young, the old,
the very old;
Men: boys, the young, the old,
the very old;
even *takumbeng* with displayed greying
groins and sagging breasts,
for a curse;
All violated the scorching sun
to say enough is enough,
to the ruins of a
once popular political dream:
Le R E N O U V E A U!
With their guns on the ready
a lone miserable 'copter splashing
away in the sky, raining tear-gas
Bamenda had gone berserk,
enough was enough
Bamenda *chop fire*.

31

Bamenda *chop fire*:
The soldiers, the tear-gas canisters,
the grenades, amputated limbs,
disappeared husbands and sons,
the rape of daughters and mothers
before parents, husbands, children,
brothers and sisters alike;
the whips, drinking of military urine,
bathing in dust in Sunday-white communion
garments, all to break the will of the people.
Like rocks they let the stream of soldiers
have their fill; the provocation,
all to make them fight back that the dreaded
lot be *heroshimaed* failed;
congratulations my people for knowing
when to react and when to hold your patience.
The will of the people is supreme,
virtue will always laugh last,
even if "God cannot change the results…"
Bamenda *chop fire*.

Bamenda *chop fire*:
Even though we continue to labour in vain,
dusty roads for the dry season,
muddy gullies for the rainy season,
frequently interrupted power supply,
high water bills,
belated salaries, if any at all,
while alienated leaders fly above our plight;
even though the U.N. with her devil's alternative
may not react until pools of blood begin to flow,
we have made our point.
We are the minority indeed,
but if your bastard mentor could go,
then you will surely go too.
Time is the ultimate judge
and the will of the suffering masses
the path of justice.
Bamenda *chop fire*.

Rain Clouds

That face of the earth,
the sky, bright and radiant,
then anger rises, the cloud
darkens and the thunder
rumbles and, like the
locomotive engine, gives steam
to the thick black clouds.

Gently this train glides out
of its station, heading, for
the onlooker, to an unknown
destination. But the frown on
that face is unmistaken as
the rain clouds like wrinkles converge.
Unable to accommodate it any more,
the steam is let loose and
the tears flow freely
flooding away the wrinkles from
the face of the earth.

Christmas Atem Ebini

Freedom We Wrote

As the trumpet of victory sounds
Announcing a hard won freedom
Regained from the thieves in the night
Masked in false prophetic virtue.
We dreamed in the hearts of nights
And spoke in the heats of noons
But still wrote in the chill of mornings
Of the sound of victory's trumpet.

We believed in sunshine
Even through the heavy rains;
We believed in happiness
Though going through the pains;
We believed in a bright future
Though the past and present be gloomy.
Our hands were stretched in friendship
Our love for fatherland was paramount.
The enemy threw a deadly fist
To distort the meaning of our message,
And yet we dreamt, wrote and spoke
Of a time to come
Different from today and yesterday;
A tomorrow with the trumpets sound
Announcing our hard-won freedom
Based on **the freedom we wrote.**

Bernard Nsokika Fonlon

The Fear of the Future Years

Oft, in my cheerless hour,
When, in my soul, 'tis stormy,
I see dread Failure's lour
O'erhang the years before me;
      For, then, it seems
      The cherished dreams
That urge my youthful strife,
      And make me strain,
      In sun and rain,
Must end a wasted life.

Thus, in my cheerless hour,
When, in my soul, 'tis stormy,
I see dread Failure's lour
O'erhang the years before me.

Great men, the stories say,
Oft also stood uncertain
Of what before them lay,
Behind the Future's curtain;
      But forging on,
      Their end they won,
While God illumed their way;
      And buoyed by this,
      I feel some bliss,
For he's my Light and Stay.

Still, in my cheerless hour,
When, in my soul, 'tis stormy,
I see dread Failure's lour
O'erhang the years before me.

I see my dying bed,
The futile years behind it,
A life all fruitless led,

With scarce a soul to minf it;
　　Those hopes absurd,
　　In youth, that spurred,
All shrunk like fountains dried;
　　One thing alone
　　Allays my moan –
The thought that I had tried.

Thus, in my cheerless hour,
When, in my soul, 'tis stormy,
I see dread Failure's lour
O'erhang the years before me.

Gem of the Highlands

'Tis the scene of my Homeland
　　So charming in May;
O wild was thy beauty,
　　When young was my day;
How pranced the gay streamlet
　　O'er upland and fen!
How thrilling this blending!
　　Of mountain and glen.

Gone, the wild scapes of yestreen,
　　Gone the once roaring linn!
With tillage ever spreading
　　The streamlet is thin.
Where the clansman was ready
　　To die for the Fon,
A new hustings liar
　　Puts peace on the run.

May the fierce deadly Levin
　　Wipe out this domain;
May the ties that bound fondly
　　Bind us once again;
Let the ashes of discord
　　Be buried in urn;

May thy clansman as yestreen
  Rove free o'er bank and burn.

Thy bonnie braes, Homeland,
  So charming I May,
How weird was your beauty,
  When young I was gay;
Meandered your streamlets
  Pas upland and fen;
How thrilling this blending
  Of Mountain and glen!

Bongasu Tanla Kishani

A Native Song

With the cue
Below the crane
We took it up to resound
Holy Holy, Ho…
But with a solemn whetted voice
They slashed it off
Drumming it evenly
And curbing it duly
In a know tongue,
As we gaped unto the end.
Then I felt a sacred chill
Slowly blowing in
And hovering over us
It enveloped us
Within those marble walls
Of our Roman shrine
In the silence that reigned.
And on our knees,
We scanned the sacred folds
Unfolding the mysterious fold:
A renewing plea to love
With drums and clanging cymbals.

The Eternal Tatoo

Brother hark!
Tiptoeing around the blooming fields
And tethering the reins of our embers
I sow seeds because I'm a crop.

I abandon the laughing crowd
to weave new riddles
Out from the dancing crowd
We fell the mahogany
to lay a new xylophone set
We searched for leather for a new drum
We survey a new play-ground for a juvenile dance
Our embers never grow poor
Our xylophone never wears out.

Fallen woods from untrodden fields
Our xylophone – a ladder bridging every note
It bridges our age to ancestral drumming
We bridge the woods, fallen and unfallen
As heralds of a common lore.

Brother hark!
This is my prophecy:
The tattoos of our lives smoulder on
From the seeds you sow
from the riddles you weave
from the dry skin that crowns the drum
crackles a crop of our era's craft
The tattoos of an age never smoulder away.

The blooming fields, the dancing folk
are green embers with bridles in our hands
I till with the spade of hope
and sing with the voice of faith
in a sprouting Manjong chorus
because I'm a crop.

Buma Kor

One Fine Morning

Early in the morning
When the sky begins to clear
and the animal world is awake,
I see the sun rising and
I hear the noise of a new day.

I see people waking with new burdens
and people continuing with old strives
I see young one struggling to establish
and old ones on the verge of decay;
I see wizards from night manoeuvres
and witches and evil-doers at work.

I do not see a bit of the good old day
but a new day, new things and new troubles
when darkness descends.

I see it overshadowing the new things
and the new things become old again
and nobody seems to take notice of them,
because it is normal for them to come and go.
How I long for another morning!

The Coming of the Waves

Rolling rolls of water
rolling to the shore
stormed in the wind
the foam paving the way,
swiftly flow the waves.

Whatever they bring
is witnessed by who they meet;
rolling rolls of water.

What good can they bring
from distant seas?
We ought to wait to see
rolling rolls of water
rolling to the shore.

The waiter cannot any longer
mayhaps no good comes;
save that I see in my mind

Rolling rolls of water to the shore.

      roll on
      gentle water of the advent

      roll on
      unseen things perceived of

      roll on my patent hopes
      to the shores of my mind.

I am the water of the waves
I can see the foam oozing
but the current is high
the current is still high.

Silhouette

I see two hills in a mist
Hidden in the horizon;
Between them is a gorge
Like an open wound.

They rise and collapse like banana trees
The wind against them is strong
Their base is strewn with refuse and mud
Their tops are concealed in clouds of grief.

Who will take the case for these twin-hills?
Who will recreate the created bliss?
Have those hills real sons and daughters?
Who will rebuild the nation's statecraft?

The answer comes through the oceans
Faintly but tremendously backed:
The hills shall not live without aid
They cannot live by themselves!

When this combat in me is over
And the concatenation of highlands known
Then I shall come to see the end
Between two hills.

Patrick Sam Kubam

The Last Legacy

When my grandmother was to depart,
She smiled to me,
"Sweet child, I am leaving you,
But before I go, I must
Reveal to you the knowledge of your ancestors,
The treasure which shall be your guiding star."

"Mother," I coughed, "I will willingly listen."
And thus she spoke to me:

Never annoy a woman with a broom
In her hand, for if she beats you with it,
You shall become impotent.
Whenever you see the rainbow
Encircle the sun, know that
A king will die.
If a cock should stand at the door
And crow, know that it is announcing
The death of a close relative.
If ever a cock should lay an egg in your house,
Be thankful, for God shall shower
Gifts on you and you shall have twins.
When the owl hoots on top of your house,
Know that a witch or a wizard
Is asking you to pay a debt,
Either in money or human flesh.
If ever you see a kite hover
In the air on one spot,
Know that someone close to you
Is sick. And if the kite dives
Towards the earth,
Stop whatever you are doing,
For you have lost someone dear to you.
When you feel a twitching of your eye-lid

Know that you shall see a dead body.
A twitching of your foot indicates
That you shall go on a journey.
One in your thigh means that
You shall lie with a woman.
When you feel a twitching of your tongue,
Beware of your enemies;
You shall have a quarrel and a fight.
And, my son, if you feel a twitching
Of your elbow, know that you shall
Help in the burial of someone.

"Mother, right now I feel a twitching
Of my eye-lid and of my elbow.
Whet does this forebode?" I muttered.

And my grandmother has not replied
Up till now; but lies reposing in her tomb.

Sankie Maimo

The Bugle Call

Harken boys, to the bugle call.
'Tis a stern summons for all.
Leave off all forms of play;
Come, take your 'worthy pay'.

The Nation rewards with immortality,
The youths who suffer such indignity
In braving the task of reconstruction.
Smile boys, for you've made a 'shining' contribution.

Forget not your duties at all
Tho' sworn wretches undermind and forestall
Every honest effort you make.
Smile lads, even at the stake.

The day of reckoning shall down.
Broken, the wretches daren't you penalise
For your dream will then materialise.
Smile boys, for then you'll wear your crown.

The Harvest

Come down, brother,
From that lofty mountain-height,
Where thunder breaks and roars
With fire and brimstone.
Come away, for a while
And lock the gates against devastating floods.

Come down, brother,
From yonder cheery dream-land
With lotus fruit galore,
Where sirens laugh and sing;
Come away, for a while
And tend the seedlings in the rich green fields.
Descend, big brother,
From your lofty mountain-top
Where incense burns and charms!
Off your silk and rich taffeta!
Come away for a while
And, from the refuse-heap, pick up an angel.

Judgement

The flower that blooms at the door
Fascinates the bee
And charms the spider;
       With aroma
       Sublime…
Invites all the world,
But it is lonely and in blossom.
Now, go seek it,
And tell me all about beauty.

The bird that sings on the hedge
Chatters now to the mob
And warbles to the vagabond
       In notes
       Mysterious…
Chanting a wearied town-crier.
Yet it is alone, the only messenger.
Now go seek it,
And give proof of your wisdom.

But beyond the rich hedge-rows,
Down in the streets, along the alleys,
Benefactors, rich in giles and wiles,
       With faces
       Celestial…
Besiege every stronghold and fortification.
They come in battalions with clanging cymbals;
Some serenade, but others carry averruncators.
Hence question not the present oracle.

Though weary after an experience
Below the stairs, the angels have supped
All night with the long-eared ass;
       To the beat
       Of the tam-tam…
In answer to the leopard dance.
If the wolves and the hyenas now threaten,
You'll never drive them from the door

51

For the lion underwent a heart operation.

From now, you'll ever be on trial.
With the blind eight-eyed spider discredited,
The bee now heralds the mythological change.
        Witness the nomination!
        A flower for the bee!
Blest with its honey, its eternal charm,
Here are the sacred paraphernalia
Of the new oracle of your native soil.
Now, mate, question not its efficacy.

John Menget

I Gree

I gree for my mami
I gree for my papa
I gree for my mama yi mami
I gree for my papa before my papa
For sika my head.

And dat my head na big house,
Wey mami and papa been build'am for me;
Inside de head na book,
Dat book, na power
And power be ALL.

I salute my mami
I salute my papa,
And de man wey make we all
Na yi make me more
I gree for God.

Ba'Bila Mutia

Dilemma of a Supermarket

Location: Yaounde

Impute yourself now
Bi-pedalled yaks,
Adorned in money-hungry
Shylock-garbs, fetid
Overcoats of greed and
Replenish your pockets with

Hard-acquired gold of
Perspiring ragged peasants.

When the gong of
Nemesis sounds its tolls
Not even the prophet's presence
Will save you,
You and your chalk-skinned
Vin rouge kinsmen,
From reduction to
Caustic congeries of malignity,
Oedematous rumpus of laical animus.

Let the prophet be absent

And taste not the
Over-sour egress,
Vengeful vent of overburdened spleens

Nor the double-angered
Fierceness of fiery falchions.

Germanus Canisius Nchanji (1940)

A Tale of Lalang Grass

It was… the green shoots of lalang grass
    Sparked a vain hope in my breast.
So young in bud among the stubs of burnt shrubs,

    They sang, the epic of bloated days.
She knew the whistle even in the fiercest wind,
      Ridge after ridge she'd leap for joy
      She said she hated to be coy.
By the river a few bees hummed their lyrics
For us alone; she kisses me till I almost melt.
    But the sun cast our shadow in the earth,
    The village séance spelled in sternest tones,
    "This love must die; ye are eighth cousins!"

    It was the greenness of their youth,
      Supple, Glaucous,
    Turgid with the first drops of summer rain,
      Nimble, burgeoning,
    Tilting the earth where the ashes clotted,
    Ready to pierce and hurt.
    It is the lalang grass that chases me
    Like a swarm of bees in all my dreams.

Woman On A Skiff In The Ndian River

    Where are you heading,
  Woman on a skiff, paddle in hand
    Plying the brackish water?
Where are you heading with grey tufted hair
    Early in the morning
  With the darkness lingering
    Licking the water
  No weaver birds yet twittering
    Where are you heading?

What awesome mission weights
Compels the heart to adventure
Alone from your warm thatched hut
Into the cold current of the Ndian River?
Away from hot glowing coals at the hearth
Away from the smoke lingering at twilight?
What mission propels on the solo drive
Defying age, challenging the dark depths
The sun's about to peep on the glassy mass.
What urgent rendezvous do you have to meet
You've shrugged off sweet morning sleep,
A giddy heart not wanting to tarry
Nor kill time as palm trees stand
Sentinels along the river course!

Where are you heading?
Heavy rollers of our speed boat
Rush in at you in rapid succession
By God! You know the water
As you know the back of your hand;
You understand its element, what empowerment!
Got the eye of an eagle.
Intent on killing the approaching wave
A lean of the paddle, a steadying of the skiff
A wriggle on your sitting place
Now raised to the crest…
It is paddle, paddle, paddle!

Now swallowed into limbo…
Now up and clear into heaven
There you go: only minor ripples re-echo
As you continue, head high, unperturbed
Heading for the mangrove creeks?
Heading for where the fish will bite
Heading for the high seas?
Where are you heading?

Juliana Makuchi Nfah

Seasons

When leaves begin to fall
And the trees almost bared,
With gusts of blinding sandy winds
Here and there;

Brown lifeless monotonous scenery,
Hard, cracked, red laterite,
Hungry faces and cracked lips and soles,
Hot, sweating, brown-tanned bodies
With quenchless throats,
Announce the severe harmattan.

As dark clouds spread over the sky
It becomes less hot.
Whirlwinds and apparent darkness,
Heavy raindrops and hailstone
Hit bare-skinned children
Striving for some of those precious stones;
Old men over a calabash if wine,
Women chat around an evening fire.

A people to sleep quietly go,
Noisy unwanted mosquitoes
Freshly come from swamps and slums
Mercilessly inject their deadly juice
Into human skins.

Such, if we recall,
Are some hazards and joys
Encountered when the skies
Mourn the death of a lost one.

Sunset on the Waves

The breeze came gently soothing
Caressing the little waves
Urging them on towards the shore,
And I knew a cool tender feeling.

As I stood consumed by that mood
I saw the golden rays of the setting sun
With timidly outstretched fingers touch
The lovely waves of the great expanse of water.

They now advanced at regular intervals,
The waves. Murmuring with the hum of bees
A melody that hastened the steps of a traveller
Obliged to tarry in awe, in admiration.

They now curled in, the waves,
Like an army of snakes riding to battle;
And on them, swaying in dance admirable,
Rode the boats of fishermen and villagers.

They were gliding along, the boats,
In stately dance to the melody of the waves.
And what greenery around them!
Of distant trees in the horizon.

Trees standing in stately pattern
Of the half-moon, their branches in
Humble bow, over the water, like mother
Over her crying baby, to the sun-god.

There I stood gazing in awe
At the boats and their men
The trees and their half-circle
The riding waves and the golden rays.

I knew not dusk was setting in
When came from within the pronouncement:
There is nothing so beautiful as the rays of

The setting sun on a moving body of water.

Ngong Kum Ngong (   )

Medicinal Brandy

Songs are medicinal
though they sometimes draw tears.
Diseased hearts rise to their feet
and tethered minds find their tongues.
Burdened breasts weep tears of joy
and ulcers slay their maggots
to leap to the defence of invalids.

Lyrics are curative agents
thought they sometimes exasperate.
Lunatics screech like doped monkeys
and swindlers sway into action.
Imprisoned reason jerks in glee
and prejudice ponders patching
to raise bigotry to a new status.

I will sing all day like birds,
travelling along the land
like a troubadour in love.
Since songs are medicinal,
curing morbid conditions
to cleanse the land of putrefaction,
I invite you all naked like stones
to think seriously about your disease.

Medicinal brandy revives the soul,
makes people perceive and perform better
though it sometimes hatches revolutions
sticking out its neck for legality.
I invite you all quaking with terror
to destroy fear with medicinal brandy
and cleanse every home teeming with mosquitoes.

Wonderful Artist

I love watching weaver birds
from the stool of my mission.
I love watching these artists
weaving and singing merrily
resolved chic houses to construct
for the unhatched, their future prop.

Cobras excavate the place
looking for newly hatched eggs.
Mambas deadly charms concoct
to benumb the minds of builders
resolved like weaver birds to build.
Scorpions from place to place saunter
determined to poison every dream
we nurse to liberate our country.

I enjoy watching weaver birds
from the castle of my conscience.
I enjoy watching these architects
moulding with care their tomorrow
while like vultures man makes merry
feeding fat on the flesh of kinsmen.

I like watching these wonderful artists
forging in harmony their destiny
like infuriated black soldier ants
resolved to crush any invading foe.

The Handwriting

Those that survived now have grown tough
the fishes you once fed on
while hunger preyed on our muscles.
It is now thirsty, bubbling within,
the lake you took pleasure fishing in.
Incense of death bloodthirsty eagle
suffocates our sense of sympathy.
Those that survived have also established,
the small fishes you enjoyed baiting
while thirst battered our dehydrated souls.
They have sealed their ears with paraffin wax
so peruse the handwriting on the wall.

I see fright in your hawkish eyes,
the ravenous greed and hunger
like a female praying mantis
biting deep into your underbelly
crying, craving more plasma to survive.
Incense of damnation wrinkled donkey
blisters even the tongues of praise singers.
so peruse the handwriting on the wall.

John Nkemngong Nkengasong (1959)

Mfoundi Faery

Sweet dame, sweet woman in her prime
You cannot see how stars gaze in wonder
That lovely bloom of yours
Till they are shaken out of wits
And the sun has taken sudden flight

Sweet woman symbol of god
You cannot know what anguish this hour bears
You cannot hear the clatter
And the clang of falling walls
The boom! Boom! Bang! Of the rifles
And the wullillilliying of dying voices
For the Arch Artist stowed
His idol on holy ground
Far, far away from misery

Sweet woman, O blossom night
Your glossy laps have shamed the moon
And that luster on your lips
Once withered the rose of tyranny
Your breath, that gentle morning breeze
Engendered life
And poets smiled like lunatics

Come to me, woman of my dream
And mould my rending heart
Come to me, woman of my soul
And give it respite from meditation
Come to me procurer of my soul
And haul me to your Eden, O bright Eternity!

And she came to me, vendor of my soul
And she came to me, woman of my doom
And she came to me, O dark eternity

No embittered soul broke the damp
Of salty sorrows as now I do
Knowing one thing: beauty wears daggers.

In The Toilet

I come, Invisible Presence
to your shrine
in obeisance to your call
bowel-crammed and mind-blistered
with fevers from the world

Squatted in the marble sanctuary
consumed
in a ritual of purgation
of self and soul
eyelids closed against the door
to battered life

and amidst the fretful farts
and the gleeful groans
dream piles upon dream

dream piles upon dream
till self and soul resume a dialogue
and lines of verse come dancing
in my eye
singing songs of Truth, of Bliss

Invisible Master Initiate
though I go from hence
chaste and pure
let the jolting lines of prose sojourn
so I can spread your precious gift
in the eyes of the world.

Wailing In The Jungle

Will no one listen to the silent cries
From shanties choked with th'offending
                    midnight breeze
The scythes of oppression whirling in the wind
And the venom of corruption searing
                    in plebian blood

It is a cataclysm of terror and misery
With slaves in tyrants' garbs
                    turned amuck
Turned rodents in the barns of fruitful
                    motherland
Will no one listen to them cry

No one listens to the tortured infant wail
No one hears its pitying mother's sigh
No one heeds to the farm-farer's groan
                    in this desolate jugle

The Jogglers of State are at banquet
Browsing in foreign laps
They will return like nabobs
After our little wells are drained
And swear that all is fine
Though we chaff in our misery

> *nevermore, Fuandem, nevermore*
> *nevermore the milky dawns*
> *of your shrine's shores*
> *the rhythm of your gong drowns*
> *and the water of mighty Mungo dries*
> *and want of drink, the humble's cry*
> *is life in death*
> *and death in life*
> *in my blind and bitter fatherland.*

Susan Nkwentie

Twilight

How beautiful it is to watch the
    sky slowly changing,
To watch God's power at work
    in the heavens
And wish you were one of
    the clouds
Racing across the earth's spacious
    ceiling
Watched by the lovers of nature
    while they ponder its mysteries.

The blood-red sun sinking on the
    horizon
Like a shy bright-faced girl
    covering half her face
From view, thinking she's hidden
    herself
But the rays piercing through the
    clouds betray
The hiding gestures of the
    shy girl.

Then the sluggish night slowly
    engulfs the earth
In its enormous cloak of
    incomprehensible mystery
And nature switches on its
    twinkling lights
And the ungrateful humans put
    on their street lamps
As if nature, rather than God
    created stars.

The insects begin chirping in tune
    to nature's music
And the accursed humans disturb
    peace and sweetness
With their booming nonsense, blaring
    through the shop windows
And the wind carries the sound to
    the peaceful suburbs,
Disturbing the serenity with an
    an anxious uneasy boom.
And twilight slowly turns to dark…

The Early Rains

I looked through the window
And the sky was grey with nimbus clouds
Obscuring the rays of the sun.
It seemed the heavens were at odds;
Then a mighty wind arose from the East
And among the trees made a sound like
A horde of bees in motion.

Then came the huge drops
Drumming on the zinc roofs
Like jigitta beads
On a dancing woman's hips.
Finally down it came in showers:
It poured and swept and waited
As if from an unseen tower
By a maid unleashed in anger.

Everything was swallowed in the murk
The distant hills became illusions
And the very houses became barely visible.
Then it stopped; like a screen withdrawn,
From before my watching eyes.
The trees all fresh and green
The leaves waving gladly.

The juicy pear with drops of water
Reflecting in the evening sun like pearls,
The air cool and refreshing
After the blazing heat of the day.
And so it will be in the night for sleepy brains
Wander over an endless sea of thoughts.

Mesack Fongang Takere

Weaverbirds

In the morning, early and bright,
Old palms stand out stripped and bare
Along this winding road
That leads away from town.
They bear golden fruits of nests
You would little dare to count.

These architects in their subtle numbers,
Excited each in his own way,
Chat busily, in ecstasy of delight,
Glad they were born a happier race
To hail greetings across to each other,
In melody and a thousand chirping noises.

Each weaver-friend of mine
Would often and again fly,
Breaking company to some distant place,
And swiftly returns with a leafy thread
To entwine into yet another nest,
A perfect home, cosy and beautiful.

They shout loudly and make inquiries
About good health and easy living,
Swearing promises to exchange gifts.
This I envy and make an approach;
But the whole colony, down to a man,
Fly themselves far and away.

Pitt Tah Tawang

Great Cattle Egret

Hail back here!
Great Cattle Egret
Poised in the vast green
On your long yellow legs
That in flight fold to the beak.

Where have you been this last season
While the skies poured their rains
To wash us clean
And our fathers
And our mothers
And our farmlands
And our plants
And our glass?

Were you there
Where the people are as white as you are?
Where the soil is as white
In the rains as your down?
Where the cattle have no lice
For your neck like a snake to gulp down?
Where the smoke from factories
Is so black and thick it blocks
In mid-air your lovely lofty flight?

And now have you come
To spend with us
These sunny days
Gliding from field to field
Your round eyes sharp
For the brow that breeds cattle?

But talk to me, Cattle Egret,
About this far-off land:

Its people and their ways,
Are they as white as your down
Or as yellow as your legs
Or as red as the rims of your eyes?

Do their kids sing and dance
Under a young moon
Round as a thumb-nail crescent?

Do they tell stories around an evening fire
Or drink palm-wine
After the day's work is done?
Tell me, great traveller,
All about these people
Who welcome you
When our harmless thunder storms
Scare you from our midst.

Patrick Tata (   )

Immaculate Feet

Coal brands flung white hot
Bang this night stained mantle cap
To this shy tyrant's baton lash I beat
And steam with the tickled land,
Victim of fury, brunt of bashes carpy

Then heaven's face frowns black from blue,
Roars the yawning crackles of white fire,
Zipping the skies, cannon cracked bullets
A thousand spears spray, splat and torrent,
Cascading on floured earth in rush,
Jumbling all looseness to scrambled eggs
Splashed with chaffs, rags, broken bits, baggings,
Bottles gashed and tangle-merged with
Zebra dung, and foods and skunk flavours…

This is town heart of man and nature tart
Nose-clogging, gut sickening to the finicky
And this ruthless rustle of city rush needs hype
Fine-tuned, sonorous and sleek
Of this pavement street guard, gutter filler
Forgotten in the sea-rush rough speed…
Where do I step immaculate feet to spare my ward?

The Teacher

When in this can of worms nauseous mates,
Worms, all worms wallow in the filth of ventral debts,
The teacher wings with the eagle
Pulses with the quasar
A worm with a difference

A Glow-Worm blighting the sun's blaze
Glowing in the darkness of ignorant-cence
When the cowardly sun fails;
He is the sun of innocence.

Some nights scare the moon of borrowed beams
As the racing sun razes her blinking gleams
And the teacher shines always
With inborn radiance
While stars thrill with quivering winks
From untouchable heights of unconcern
The teacher is at home here
Affably available for all.

All the lamps of smart life
From bushfires to neon lights
Fire-lighting the callings of men
Have not touched the heart of innocence
Like the teacher's fire-fly pulses.

The teacher is a winged quasar
No man-rigged glory compares
Nor shouting sun nor smiling moon nor winking stars
All so dumb, all dusty.

Professing or born, the teacher is a brainstorm
To earthy grubs, to bonfires, to wayfarers
The teacher is the Pole Star-Worm
Guiding innocence, lighting ignorance
And we have not sung him yet.

Mathew Takwi

When Shall We Dance

When shall we wriggle
Our thread-waists to dying
Tunes of election misappropriation?

When shall we twist
Our punctured bodies to end songs
Of clan appointees to high offices?

When shall we tongue-twist
To fallen awkward glimmerings
Of junta sycophants?

When shall we stop yawning
With cracked lips over flat stomach and
Gracefully fox-trot in our evergreen land?

When shall we blues to ebbing sounds
Of unmasked tax evaders hemmed as
Ruling party barons, while the treasury dries up?

When shall we rumba to
Rhythms of a collapsed king and shout:
"At last! At last! We have been unchained
From bondage?"

Cherished Devil

When his cannons
Laid steel eggs:
Breaths extinguished.

When triggers jerked
And barrels vomited:
Arms and limbs like
Ball bounced.

With the land carpeted
With red human fuel;
His enemy brother rushed in
Brandishing a barrled placard.

Now!
With this fire eyed chaser around
And icy silence sensed;
He drained cash lakes.

Like little chased mouse,
Brief hideout was sought at neighbour's-
Dark continent's triangular Land.

There!
Love for this devil's disciple
Superseded hatred.

Wherefrom,
He headed for the unknown:
His hand-made cage.

Twin Streams

Twin streams rise from black tops
Of white round twin hills,
Encircled by tall black grass
Flow in straight twin directions,
Down smooth kapok twin lands
To be carried by hand of cloth.

Twin sweet streams that flow only
When the land is cemented with wrath,
When the land groans in pains
Or,
When the land vibrates in mirth,
Always rise with an explosive start.

See twin son's of Africa's bilingual pierce
With twin tongues of Voltaire and Shakespeare,
With Voltaire's half-son trampling on brother always
For him to know the stream of wrath and pain only;
Breathing!
What a complex issue.

Fale Wache

Lament of a Mother

(Adapted from the Noni original)
(Extract)

Ndikochong, my son, my husband
My father, my all,
Thirty long years since you left us
Thirty weary years you've been away from us
Your silence sends daggers through my heart
I'm miserable.
My man, how could you, can you,
Do this to me, your mother?
I who breast-fed you with my turgescent milk
Beguenthed you that angelic smile
Those milk-white pearly teeth
And, little truant, when you got naughty,

I admit, I spanked you
But at the same time, I soothed you,
Carrying you on my back, chanting lullabies
To lull you to sleep
And you slept.

Ndikochong, my son, is it you
Who has done this to me?
Thirty years and the tears have
Flowed like the *Kibin* river at the
Peak of the rainy season

We have waited
With hushed breadth
For your return
Every new day when the Sun wakes
We wash our eyes and
Wait and watch

But nobody comes
And our hearts are heavy.

Ndikochong, come back
Come back, my son, named after
My father.
Come back and lift
This hammer of
Pain that pounds on our hearts.
My man, my husband,
Scalding tears cut ridges
Down my furrowed face,
Sleepless nights on frightful days.
My eyes riveted on the road
Day and night watching
Return... Return...

They say you went in search of
Knowledge and Wisdom
Tell me: did you have to abandon
Your kith and kin
Sit in that gargantuan noisy eagle-bird
Soar over seas, oceans, rivers
Mountains and nebulous clouds
Just to acquire knowledge?

Where did the venerable Ba Ndong go
To acquire Knowledge?
Where did the celebrated Ba Ndong go
To glean Learning?
Where did the patriarch Ba Ndong go
To possess Wisdom?
Ans wasn't he the sagest man
That was ever heard about
From where the sun rises to where it sleeps?

No, no, no my son
Not wisdom but a
Devious scheme to torment
Your own and send them to a premature

Death…

Your friends took up lucrative jobs
Took care of their ailing parents
Helped their brothers and sisters
But you?
No, not you; you must drink
All the volumes and volumes of books tat
Have ever been printed.

Of what use is that book?
Of what use is that book-intoxicated skull of yours
If our hollow stomachs sempiternally
Growl and groan?
Remember Bolame?
The nubile lass with the thrusting
Breasts and the heaving bosom
The scintillating village belle with the ample
Backside and the necklace that sparkled
Like stars on a moonless night
In the village playground.

Remember Bolame?
How men's mouths watered at her sight?

Ten years since you left us
Ten years since you've been away
She has
Flowered
Blossomed
Bloomed.
Lecherous eyes
Guileful tongues
Hunger for the succulent
Fruit.

Ndikochong, my own,
Your father carried a colossal calabash
Of frothing Palm Wine to her parents
And they drank in your name.

Now the poor girl complains she can no longer wait:
Other importune her and her womanhood wails for solace.

How long, she inquires, how long
Shall I have to wait
For a husband so far away? Maybe
He is married and no longer needs me.

Come Ndikochong, return my son
And take your coveted bride
Before the vulturous predatory-men
Swoop down and scoop her away.
Return Ndikochong and take your resplendent
Bride with the
Sooth-black glossy hair
Ebony velvety skin
Ivory teeth with a door in the middle
That when open sends several men crazy.
My eyes itch to see my grandchildren
My ears yearn to listen to their shouts and cries
My hands long to cradle and rock them
My back hungers to strap and carry them
Before I depart to meet my fathers in the
Next world.

II

AFRICA

Koffi Awoonor

Songs of Sorrow

Dzogbese Lisa has treated me thus
It has led me among the sharps of the forest
Returning is not possible
And going forward is a great difficulty
The affairs of this world are like the chameleon faeces
Into which I have stepped
When I clean it cannot go.

I am on the world's extreme corner,
I am not sitting in the row with the eminent
But those who are lucky
Sit in the middle and forget
I am on the world's extreme corner
I can only go beyond and forget.

My people, I have been somewhere
If I turn here, the rain beats me
If I turn there the sun burns me
The firewood of this world
Is for only those who can take heart
That is why not all can gather it.
The world is not good for anybody
But you are so happy with your fate;
Alas! the travellers are back
All covered with debt.

Something has happened to me
The things so great that I cannot weep;
I have no sons to fire the gun when I die
And no daughters to wail when I close my mouth
I have wondered on the wilderness
The great wilderness men call life
The rain has beaten me,
And the sharp stumps cut as keen as knives

I shall go beyond and rest.
I have no kin and no brother,
Death has made war upon our house;

And Kpeti's great household is no more,
Only the broken fence stands;
And those who dared not look in his face
Have come out as men.
How well their pride is with them.
Let those gone before take note
They have treated their offspring badly.
What is the wailing for?
Somebody is dead. Agosu himself
Alas! a snake has bitten me
My right arm is broken,
And the tree on which I lean is fallen.

Agosi if you go tell them,
Tell Nyidevu, Kpeti, and Kove
That they have done us evil ;
Tell them their house is falling
And the trees in the fence
Have been eaten by termites;
That the martels curse them.
Ask them why they idle there
While we suffer, and eat sand.
And the crow and the vulture
Hover always above our broken fences
And strangers walk over our portion.

John Pepper Clark

Olokun

I love to pass my fingers,
As tide through weds of the sea
And wind the tall fern-fronds
Through the strands of your hair
Dark as night that screens the naked moon:

I am jealous and passionate
Like Jehovah, God of the Jews,
And I would that you realize
No greater love had woman
From man than the one I have for you!

But what wakeful eyes of man,
Made of the mud of this earth,
Can stare at the touch of sleep
The sable vehicle of dream
Which indeed is the look of your eyes?

So drunken, like ancient walls
We crumble in heaps at your feet;
And as the good maid of the sea,
Full of rich bounties for men,
You lift us all beggars to your breast.

Night Rain

What time of night it is
I do not know
Except that like some fish
Doped out of the deep
I have bobbed up bellywise
From stream of sleep
And no cocks crow.
It is drumming hard here
And I suppose everywhere
Droning with insistent ardour upon
Our roof-thatch and shed
And through sheaves slit open
To lightning and rafters
I cannot make out overhead
Great water drops are dribbling
Falling like orange or mango
Fruits showered forth in the wind
Or perhaps I should say so
Much like beads I could in prayer tell
Them on string as they break
In wooden bowls and earthenware
Mother is busy now deploying
About our roomlet and floor.
Although it is so dark
I know her practised step as
She moves her bins, bags, and vats
Out of the run of water
That like ants filing out of the wood
Will scatter and gain possession
Of the floor. Do not tremble then
But turn brothers, turn upon your side
Of the loosening mats
To where the others lie.
We have drunk tonight of a spell
Deeper than the owl's or bat's
That wet of wings may not fly.
Bedraggled upon the *iroko*, they stand
Emptied of hearts, and

Therefore will not stir, no, not
Even at down for then
They must scurry in to hide.
So we'll roll over on our back
And again roll to the beat
Of drumming all over the land
And under its ample soothing hand
Joined to that of the sea
We will settle to sleep of the innocent.

Agbor Dancer

See her caught in the throb of a drum
Tippling from hide-brimmed stem
Down lineal veins to ancestral core
Opening out in her supple tan
Limbs like fresh foliage in the sun.

See how entangled in the magic
Maze of music
In trance she treads the intricate
Pattern rippling crest after crest
To meet the green clouds of the forest.

Tremulous beats wake trenchant
In her heart a descant
Tingling quick to her finger tips
And toes virginal habits long
Too atrophied for pen or tongue.

Could I, early sequester'd from my tribe,
Free a lead-tether'd scribe
I should answer her communal call
Lose myself in her warm caress
Intervolving earth, sky and flesh.

Susan Lwanga

Daybreak

O dawn
Where to you hide your paints at night
Tha cool breath, that scent,
With which you sweeten the early air?

O dawn
What language do you use
To instruct the birds to sing
Their early songs
And insects to sound
The rhythm of an African heartbeat?

O dawn
Where do you find the good will
To speed the early traffic on its way,
Rouse the cold drunkard
And send your askaris and barking dogs
To chase thieves to their dens?

O dawn
Whose cold breath makes young boys and girls
Glad of a warm sheet,
Enflames the dreams of unmarried ones,
And brings familiar noises
To gladden the hearts of the married.

Oswald Mbuyiseni Mtshali

The Face Of Hunger

I counted ribs on his concertina chest
bones protruding as if chiselled
by a sculptor's hand of famine.

He looked with glazed pupils
seeing only a bun on some sky-high shelf.

The skin was pale and taut
like a glove on a doctor's hand.

His tongue darted in and out
like a chameleon's
snatching a confetti of flies.

O! child
your stomach is a den of lions
roaring day and night.

The Birth Of Shaka

His baby cry
was of a cub
tearing the neck
of the lioness
because he was fatherless.

The gods
boiled his blood
in a clay pot of passion
to course in his veins.

His heart was shaped into an ox shield
to foil every foe.

Ancestors forged
his muscles into
thongs as tough
as wattles bark
and nerves
as sharp as
syringa thorns.

His eyes were lanterns
that shone from the dark valleys of Zululand
to see white swallows
coming across the sea.
His cry to two assassin brothers:

"Lo! You can kill me
but you'll never rule this land!"

Christopher Okigbo

Heavensgate, I

Before you, mother Idoto,
    naked I stand;
before your watery presence,
    a prodigal
leaning on an oilbean,
lost in your legend.

Under your powder wait I
    on barefoot,
watchman for the watchword
    at *Heavensgate*;

out of the depths my cry:
give ear and hearken…

Dark waters of the beginning.

Rays, violet and short, piercing the gloom,
foreshadows the rain that is dreamed of.

Me to the orangery
solitude invites,
a wagtail, to tell
the tangled-wood-tale;
a sunbird, t mourn
a mother on a spray.

Rain and sun in single combat;
on one leg standing,
n silence at the passage,
he young bird at the passage.

Silent faces at crossroads:
    festivity in black…

Faces of black like long black
    column of ants,

behind the bell tower,
into the hot garden
where all roads meet:
festivity in black...

O Anna at the knobs of the panel oblong,
hear us at crossroads at the great hinges

where the players of loft pipe organs
rehearse old lovely fragments, alone –

strains of pressed orange leaves on pages,
bleach of the light of years held in leather:

For we are listening in cornfields
    among the wind players,
listening to the wind leaning over
    it loveliest fragment...

Lenrie Peters

Mine Is the Silent Face

Mine is the silent face
in the railway compartment
    in the queue
My flesh is drowsy with paint
    hideously faint
I travel through desperate
deserted places, my life
    ends in you vacantly
an empty tin rolling down
    catty cobbled alleys.

I know the strength of the wind
in anger and the passion of waves
    – no floating mermaids –
Standing as I do
as all do
at the cutting chaotic edge of things
my youth burrows into the yearning
entrails of earth; dessicated.

A blank image stares out of flames
out of dense affluent tomorrow
    studded with blame.
I tear at toasted locks of sunlight
reeds, parched reeds creaking in my lungs
It takes my life to hold the moon in focus.

Crushing dead glass in my strong hand
is worthless. Nothing bleeds, noting relieves
It will not melt like snow
  this emptiness, this tell I invented.

Wole Soyinka

Telephone Conversation

The price seemed reasonable, location
Indifferent. The landlady swore she lived
Off premises. Nothing remained
But self-confession. 'Madam,' I warned,
'I hate a wasted journey – I am African.'
Pressurized good-breeding. Voice, when it came,
Lipstick coated, long gold-rolled
Cigarette-holder pipped. Caught I was, foully.
'HOW DARK?' ... I had not misheard. ... 'ARE YOU LIGHT
OR VERY DARK?' Button B. Button   A. Stench
Of rancid breath of public hide-and-speak.
Red booth. Red pillar-box. Red double-tiered
Omnibus squelching tar. It *was* real! Shamed
By ill-mannered silence, surrender
Pushed dumbfoundment to beg simplification.
Considerate she was, varying the emphasis –
'ARE YOU DARK? OR VERY LIGHT?' Revelation came.
'You mean – like plain or milk chocolate?
Her assent was clinical, crushing in its light
Impersonality. Rapidly, wave-length adjusted,
I chose. 'West African sepia' – and as afterthought,
'Down in my passport.' Silence for spectroscopic
flight of fancy, till truthfulness clanged her accent
hard on the mouthpiece? 'WHAT'S THAT?' conceding
'DON'T KNOW WHAT THAT IS.' 'Like brunette.'
'THAT'S DARK, ISN'T IT?' 'Not altogether.
Facially, I am brunette, but madam, you should see
The rest of me. Palm of my hand, soles of my feet
Are a peroxide blonde. Friction, caused –
Foolishly madam – by sitting down, has turned
My bottom raven black – One moment madam!' – sensing
Her receiver rearing on the thunderclap
About my ears – 'Madam,' I pleaded, 'wouldn't you rather
See for yourself?'

Abiku

In vain your bangles cast
Charmed circles at my feet
I am Abiku, calling for the first
And the repeated time.

Must I weep for goats and cowries
For palm oil and the sprinkled ash?
Yams do not sprout in amulets
To earth Abiku's limbs.

So when the nail is burnt in his shell,
Whet the heated fragment, brand me
Deeply on the breast. You must know him
When Abiku calls again.

I am the squirrel teeth, cracked
The riddle of the palm. Remember
This, and dig me deeper still into
The god's swollen foot.

Once and the repeated time, ageless
Though I puke; and when you pour
Libations, each finger points me near
The way I came, where

The ground is wet with mourning
White dew suckles flesh-birds
Evening befriends the spider, trapping
Flies in wind-froth;

Night, and Abiku sucks the oil
From lamps. Mothers! I'll be the
Suppliant snake coiled on the doorstep
Yours the killing cry.

The ripest fruit was saddest;
Where I crept, the warmth was cloying.
In the silence of webs, Abihu moans, shaping

106

Mounds from the yolk.

IV THE BEGINNING

Low beneath rockshields, home of the Iron One
The sun had built a fire within
Earth' heartstone. Flames in fever fits
Ran in rock fissures, and hill surfaces
Were all aglow with earth's transparency
  Orisa-nla, Orunmila, Esu, Ifa were all assembled
  Defeated in the quest to fraternize with man

Worldlessly he rose, sought knowledge in the hills
Ogun the one saw it all, the secret
Veins of matter, and the circling lodes
Sango's spent thunderbolt served him a hammer-head
His fingers touched earth-core, and it yielded

  To think, a mere plague of finite chaos
  Stood between the gods and man

He made a mesh of elements, from stone
Of fire in earthfruit, the womb of energies
He made an anvil of peaks and kneaded
Red clay for his mould. In his hand the Weapon
Gleamed, born of the primal mechanic

  And this pledge he gave the heavens
  I will clear a path to man

His task was ended, he declined the crown
Of deities, sought retreat in heights. But Ire
Laid skilled siege to divine withdrawal. Alas
For diplomatic arts, the Elders of Ire prevailed;
He descended, and they crowned him king

  Who speaks to me in chance recesses
  Who guides the finger's eye

107

Now he climbs in reparation, who anointed
Godhead in carnage, O let heaven loose the bolts
Of last season's dam for him to lave his fingers
Merely, and in the heady line of blood
Vultures drown: Merely,

And in the lungstreams of depleted pastures
Earth is flattened. O the children of Ogun
Reaped red earth that harvest, rain
Is children's reeds and the sky a bird-pond
Until my god has bathed his hands

> Who brings a god to supper, guard him well
> And set his place with a long bamboo pole

Ogun is the lascivious god who takes
Seven gourdlets to war. One for gunpowder,
One for charms, two for palm wine and three
Air-sealed in polished bronze make
Storage for his sperms

My god Ogun, orphans' Shield, his home
Is terraced hills self-surmounting to the skies
Ogun path-maker, he who goes fore where other gods
Have turned. Shield of orphans, was your shield
In-spiked that day on sheltering lives?

Yet had he fled when his primal task was done
Fugitive from man and god, ever seeking hills
And rock bounds. Idanre's granite offered peace
And there he dwelt until the emissaries came –
Lead us king, and warlord.

> Who speaks to me I cannot tell
> Who guides the hammer's flight

Gods drowse in boredom, and their pity
Is easy roused with lush obsequious rites
Because the rodent nibbled somewhat at his yam,
The farmer hired a hunter, filled him with wine

And thrust a firebrand in his hand

We do not burn the woods to trap
A squirrel; we do not ask the mountain's
Aid, to crack a walnut.

III

England & America

W. H. Auden

Epilogue

'O WHERE are you going?' said reader to rider,
'That valley is fatal when furnaces burn,
Yonder's the midden whose odours will madden,
That gap is the grave where the tall return.'

'O do you imagine,' said fearer to farer,
'That dusk will delay on your path to the pass,
Your diligent looking discover the lacking
Your footsteps feel from granite to grass?'

'O what was that bird,' said horror to hearer,
'Did you see that shape in the twisted trees?
Behind you swiftly the figure comes softly,
The spot on your skin is a shocking disease?'

'Out of this house'— said rider to reader
'Yours never will' — said farer to fearer
'They're looking for you' — said hearer to horror
As he left them there, as he left them there.

William Blake (1759-1827)

Song

How sweet I roam'd from field to field,
    And tasted all the summer's pride
'Till I the prince of love beheld,
    Who in the sunny beams did glide!

He shew'd me lilies for my hair,
    And blushing roses for my brow;
He led me through his gardens fair,
    Where all his golden pleasures grow.

With sweet May dews my wings were wet,
    And Phoebus fir'd my vocal rage;
He caught me in his silken net,
    And shut me in his golden cage.

He loves to sit and hear me sing,
    Then, laughing, sports and plays with me;
Then stretches out my golden wing,
    And mocks my loss of liberty.

To The Muses

Whether on Ida's shady brow,
    Or the chambers of the East,
The chambers of the sun, that now
    From antient melody have ceas'd;

Whether in Heav'n ye wander fair,
    Or the green corners of the earth,
Or the blue regions of the air,
    Where the melodious winds have birth;

Whether on chrystal rocks ye rove,
    Beneath the bosom of the sea
Wand'ring in many a coral grove,
    Fair Nine, forsaking Poetry!

How have you left the antient love
    That bards of old enjoy'd in you!
The languid strings do scarcely move!
    The sound is forc'd the notes are few!

The Tyger

Tyger Tyger, burning bright,
In the forests of the night;
What immortal hand or eye,
Could frame thy fearful symmetry?

In what distant deeps or skies
Burnt the fire of thine eyes!
On what wings dare he aspire?
What the hand, dare seize the fire?

And what shoulder, & what art,
Could twist the sinews of thy heart?
And when thy heart began to beat,
What dread hand? & what dread feet?

What the hammer? What the chain,
In what furnace was thy brain?
What the anvil? What dread grasp,
Dare its deadly terrors clasp.

When the stars threw down their spears
And water'd heaven with their tears:
Did he smile his work to see?
Did he who made the Lamb make thee?

Tyger Tyger, burning bright,
In the forests of the night:
What immortal hand or eye,
Dare frame thy fearful symmetry?

Edmund Blunden

Almswomen

AT Quincey's moat the squandering village ends,
And there in the almshouse dwell the dearest friends
Of all the village, two old dames that cling
As close as any trueloves in the spring.
Long, long ago they passed threescore-and-ten,
And in this doll's house lived together then;
All things they have in common, being so poor,
And their one fear, death's shadow at the door.
Each sundown makes them mournful, each sunrise
Brings back the brightness in their failing eyes.

How happy go the rich fair-weather days
When on the roadside folk stare in amaze
At such a honeycomb of fruit and flowers
As mellows round their threshold; what long hours
They gloat upon their steepling hollyhocks,
Bee's balsams, feathery southernwood, and stocks,
Fiery dragon's-mouths, great mallow leaves
For salves, and lemon-plants in bushy sheaves,
Shagged Esau's-hands with five green finger-tips.
Such old sweet names are ever on their lips.
As pleased as little children where these grow
In cobbled patterns and worn gowns they go,
Proud of their wisdom when on gooseberry shoots
They stuck eggshells to fright from coming fruits
The brisk-billed rascals; pausing still to see
Their neighbour owls saunter from tree to tree,
Or in the hushing half-light mouse the lane
Long-winged and lordly.
                    But when these hours wane,
Indoors they ponder, scared by the harsh storm
Whose pelting Saracens on the window swarm,
And listen for the mail to clatter past
And church clock's deep bay withering on the blast;

119

They feed the fire that flings a freakish light
On pictured kings and queens grotesquely bright,
Platters and pitchers, faded calendars,
And graceful hour-glass trim with lavenders.

Many a time they kiss and cry, and pray
That both be summoned in the self-name day,
And wiseman linnet tinkling in his cage
End too with them the friendship of old age,
And all together leave their treasured room
Some bell-like evening when the may's in bloom.

Robert Bridges

London Snow (1880)

When men were all asleep the snow came flying,
In large white flakes falling on the city brown,
Stealthily and perpetually settling and loosely lying,
    Hushing the latest traffic of the drowsy town;
Deadening, muffling, stifling its murmurs failing;
Lazily and incessantly floating down and down:
    Silently sifting and veiling road, roof and railing;
Hiding difference, making unevenness even,
Into angles and crevices softly drifting and sailing.
    All night it fell, and when full inches seven
It lay in the depth of its uncompacted lightness
The clouds blew off from a high and frosty heaven;
    And all woke earlier for the unaccustomed brightness
Of the winter dawning, the strange unheavenly glare:
The eye marvelled – marvelled at the dazzling whiteness;
    The ear harkened to the stillness of the solemn air;
No sound of wheel rumbling nor of foot falling,
And the busy morning cries came thin and spare.
    Then boys I heard, as they went to school, calling,
They gathered up the crystal manna to freeze
Their tongues with tasting; their hands with snowballing;
    Or rioted in a drift, plunging up to the knees;
Or peering up from under the white-mossed wonder,
'O look at the trees!' they cried, 'O look at the trees!'
    With lessened load of few carts creak and blunder,
Following along the white deserted way,
A country company long dispersed asunder:
    When now already the sun, in pale display
Standing by Paul's[1] high dome, spread forth below
His sparkling beams, and awoke the stir of the day.
    For now doors open, and war is waged with the snow;
And trains of sombre men, past tale of number,

Refers to St. Paul's Cathedral in central London.

Tread long brown paths, as toward their toil they go:
    But even for them awhile no cares encumber
Their minds diverted; the daily word is unspoken,
The daily thought of labour and sorrow slumber
At the sight of the beauty that greets them, for the charm they have
broken.

Robert Browning

Meeting at Night

THE grey sea and the long black land;
And the yellow half-moon large and low;
And the startled little waves that leap
In fiery ringlets from their sleep,
As I gain the cove with pushing prow,
And quench its speed i' the slushy sand.

Then a mile of warm sea-scented beach;
Three fields to cross till a farm appears;
A tap at the pane, the quick sharp scratch
And blue spurt of a lighted match,
And a voice less loud, thro' its joys and fears,
Then the two hearts beating each to each!

Samuel Taylor Coleridge (1772-1834)

Ne Plus Ultra

Sole Positive of Night!
Antipathist of Light!
Fate's only essence! Primal scorpion rod -
The one permitted opposite of God! –
Condensèd blackness and abysmal storm
Compacted to one sceptre
Arms the Grasp enorm –
The Intercepter –
The Substance that still casts the shadow of Death! –
The Dragon foul and fell –
The unrevealable,
And hidden one, whose breath
Gives wind and fuel to the fires of Hell!
Ah! Sole despair
Of both the eternities in Heaven!
Sole interdict of all-bedewing prayer,
The all-compassionate!
Save to the Lampads Seven
Revealed to none of all the Angelic State,
Save to the Lampads Seven,
That watch the throne of Heaven!

Kubla Khan

IN Xanadu did Kubla Khan
A stately pleasure-dome decree:
Where Alph, the sacred river, ran
Though caverns measureless to man
    Down to a sunless sea.
So twice five miles of fertile ground
With walls and towers were girdled round:
And there were gardens bright with sinuous rills
Where blossom'd many an incense-bearing tree;
And here were forests ancient as the hills,
Enfolding sunny spots of greenery.

  But oh, that deep romantic chasm which slanted
Down the green hill athwart a cedarn cover!
A savage place! as holy and enchanted
As e'er beneath a waning moon was haunted
By woman wailing for her demon-lover!
And from this chasm, with ceaseless turmoil seething,
As if this earth in fast thick pants were breathing,
A mighty fountain momently was forced:
Amid whose swift half-intermitted burst
Huge fragments vaulted like rebounding hail,
Of chaffy grain beneath the thresher's flail:
And mid these dancing rocks at once and ever
It flung up momently the sacred river.
Five miles meandering with a mazy motion
Though wood and dale the sacred river ran,
The reach'd the caverns measureless to man,
And sank in tumult to a lifeless ocean:
And 'mid this tumult Kubla heard from far
Ancestral voices prophesying war!

   The shadow of the dome of pleasure
    Floated midway on the waves;
    Where was heard the mingled measure
    From the fountain and the caves.
It was a miracle of rare device,
A sunny pleasure-dome with caves of ice!

A damsel with a dulcimer
In a vision once I saw:
It was an Abyssinian maid,
And on her dulcimer she play'd,
Singing of Mount Abora.
Could I revive within me
Her symphony and song,
To such a deep delight 'twould win me,
That with music loud and long,
I would build that dome in air,
That sunny dome! those caves of ice!
And all who heard should see them there,
And should cry, Beware! Beware!
His flashing eyes, his floating hair!
Weave a circle round him thrice,
And close your eyes with holy dread,
For he on honey-dew hath fed,
And drunk the milk of Paradise.

William Collins (1721-1759)

Ode Written In 1746

HOW sleep the brave, who sink to rest,
By all their country's wishes blest!
When Spring, with dewy fingers cold,
Returns to deck their hallow'd mould,
She there shall dress a sweeter sod
Than Fancy's feet have ever trod.

By fairy hands their knell is rung;
By forms unseen their dirge is sung;
There Honour comes, a pilgrim grey,
To bless the turf that wraps their clay;
And Freedom shall awhile repair
To dwell, a weeping hermit, there!

Countee Cullen (1903-1946)

Heritage

What is Africa to me:
Copper sun of scarlet sea,
Jungle star or jungle track,
Strong bronzed men, or regal black
Women from whose loins I sprang
When the birds of Eden sang?
One three centuries removed
From the scenes his fathers loved,
Spicy grove, cinnamon tree,
What is Africa to me?

So I lie, who all day long
Want no sound except the song
Sung by wild barbaric birds
Goading massive jungle herds,
Juggernauts of flesh that pass
Trampling tall defiant grass
Where young forest lovers lie,
Plighting troth beneath the sky.
So I lie, who always hear,
Though I cram against my ear
Both my thumbs, and keep them there,
Great drums throbbing through the air.
So I lie, whose fount of pride,
Dear distress, and joy allied,
Is my somber flesh and skin,
With the dark blood dammed within
Like great pulsing tides of wine
That, I fear, must burst the fine
Channels of the chafing net
Where they surge and foam and fret.

Africa? A book one thumbs
Listlessly, till slumber comes.

Unremembered are her bats
Circling through the night, her cats
Crouching in the river reeds,
Stalking gentle flesh that feeds
By the river brink; no more
Does the bugle-throated roar
Cry that monarch claws have leapt
From the scabbards where they slept.
Silver snakes that once a year
Doff the lovely coats you wear,
Seek no covert in your fear
Lest a mortal eye should see;
What's your nakedness to me?
Here no leprous flowers rear
Fierce corollas in the air;
Here no bodies sleek and wet,
Dripping mingled rain and sweat,
Tread the savage measures of
Jungle boys and girls in love.
What is last year's snow to me,
Last year's anything? The tree
Budding yearly must forget
How its past arose or set —
Bough and blossom, flower, fruit,
Even what shy bird with mute
Wonder at her travail there,
Meekly labored in its hair.
One three centuries removed
From the scenes his fathers loved,
Spicy grove, cinnamon tree,
What is Africa to me?

So I lie, who find no peace
Night or day, no slight release
From the unremittant beat
Made by cruel padded feet
Walking through my body's street.
Up and down they go, and back,
Treading out a jungle track.
So I lie, who never quite

Safely sleep from rain at night —
I can never rest at all
When the rain begins to fall;
Like a soul gone mad with pain
I must match its weird refrain;
Ever must I twist and squirm,
Writhing like a baited worm,
While its primal measures drip
Through my body, crying, "Strip!
Doff this new exuberance.
Come and dance the Lover's Dance!"
In an old remembered way
Rain works on me night and day.

Quaint, outlandish heathen gods
Black men fashion out of rods,
Clay, and brittle bits of stone,
In a likeness like their own,
My conversion came high-priced;
I belong to Jesus Christ,
Preacher of humility;
Heathen gods are naught to me.

Father, Son, and Holy Ghost,
So I make an idle boast;
Jesus of the twice-turned cheek,
Lamb of God, although I speak
With my mouth thus, in my heart,
Do I play a double part.
Ever at Thy glowing altar
Must my heart grow sick and falter,
Wishing He I served were black,
Thinking then it would not lack
Precedent of pain to guide it,
Let who would or might deride it;
Surely then this flesh would know
Yours had borne a kindred woe.
Lord, I fashion dark gods, too,
Daring even to give You
Dark despairing features where,

Crowned with dark rebellious hair,
Patience wavers just so much as
Mortal grief compels, while touches
Quick and hot, of anger, rise
To smitten cheek and weary eyes.
Lord, forgive me if my need
Sometimes shapes a human creed.

All day long and all night through,
One thing only mist I do:
Quench my pride and cool my blood,
Lest I perish in the flood.
Lest a hidden ember set
Timber that I thought was wet
Burning like the dryest flax,
Melting like the merest wax,
Lest the grave restore its dead.
Not yet has my heart or head
In the least way realized
They and I are civilized.

Emily Dickinson

328

A bird came down the Walk —
He did not know I saw —
He bit an Angleworm in halves
And ate the fellow, raw,

And then he drank a Dew
From a convenient Grass —
And then hopped sidewise to the Wall
To let a Beetle pass —

He glanced with rapid eyes
That hurried all around —
They looked like frightened Beads, I thought —
He stirred his Velvet Head

Like one in danger, Cautious,
I offered him a Crumb
And he unrolled his feathers
And rowed him softer home —

Than Oars divide the Ocean,
Too silver for a seam —
Or Butterflies, off Banks of Noon
Leap, plashless² as they swim.

---

i.e. splashless

986

A narrow Fellow in the Grass
Occasionally rides –
You may have met Him – did you not
His notice sudden is –

The Grass divides as with a Comb –
A spotted shaft is seen –
And then it closes at your feet
And opens further on –

He likes a Boggy Acre
A Floor too cool for Corn –
Yet when a Boy, and Barefoot –
I more than once at Noon
Have passed, I thought, a Whip lash
Unbraiding in the Sun
When stooping to secure it
It wrinkled, and was gone –

Several of Nature's People
I know, and they know me –
I feel for them a transport
Of cordiality –

But never met this Fellow
Attended, or alone
Without a tighter breathing
And Zero at the Bone –
Emily Dickinson

Robert Frost

The Road Not Taken

Two roads diverged in a yellow wood,
And sorry I could not travel both
And be one traveller, long I stood
And looked down one as far as I could
To where it bent in the undergrowth;

The took the other, as just as fair,
And having perhaps the better claim,
Because it was grassy and wanted wear;
Though as for that the passing there
Had worn them really about the same,

And both that morning equally lay
In leaves no step had trodden black.
Oh, I kept the first for another day!
Yet knowing how way leads on to way,
I doubted if I should ever come back.

I shall be telling this with a sigh
Somewhere ages and ages hence:
Two roads diverged in a wood, and I –
I took the one less travelled by,
And that has made all the difference.

Mowing

THERE was never a sound beside the wood but one,
And that was my long scythe whispering to the ground.
What was it it whispered? I knew not well myself;
Perhaps it was something about the heat of the sun,
Something, perhaps, about the lack of sound—
And that was why it whispered and did not speak.
It was no dream of the gift of idle hours,
Or easy gold at the hand of fay or elf:
Anything more than the truth would have seemed too weak
To the earnest love that laid the swale in rows,
Not without feeble-pointed spikes of flowers
(Pale orchises), and scared a bright green snake.
The fact is the sweetest dream that labour knows.
My long scythe whispered and left the hay to make.

Range Finding

The battle rent a cobweb diamond-strung
And cut a flower beside a ground bird's nest
Before it stained a single human breast.
The stricken flower bent double and so hung.
And still the bird revisited her young.
A butterfly its fall had dispossessed
A moment sought in air his flower of rest,
Then lightly stooped to it and fluttering clung.
On the bare upland pasture there had spread
O'ernight 'twixt mullein stalks a wheel of thread
And straining cables wet with silver dew.
A sudden passing bullet shook it dry.
The indwelling spider ran to greet the fly,
But finding nothing, sullenly withdrew.

Robert Graves

Recalling War

Entrance and exit wounds are silvered clean,
The track aches only when the rain reminds.
The one-legged man forgets his leg of wood,
The one-armed man his jointed wooden arm.
The blinded man sees with his ears and hands
As much or more than once with both his eyes.
Their war was fought these twenty years ago
And now assumes the nature-look of time,
As when the morning traveller turns and views
His wild night-stumbling carved into a hill.

When, then, was war? No mere discord of flags
But an infection of the common sky
That sagged ominously upon the earth
Even when the season was the airiest May.
Down pressed the sky, and we, oppressed, thrust out
Boastful tongue, clenched fist and valiant yard.
Natural infirmities were out of mode,
For Death was young again: patron alone
Of healthy dying, premature fate-spasm.

Fear made fine bed-fellows. Sick with delight
At life's discovered transitoriness,
Our youth became all-flesh and waived the mind.
Never was such antiqueness or romance,
Such tasty honey oozing from the heart.

And old importances came swimming back –
Wine, meat, log-fires, a roof over the head,
A weapon at the thigh, surgeons at call.
Even there was a use again for God –
A word of rage in lack of meat, wine, fire,
In ache of wounds beyond all surgeoning.

War was return of earth to ugly earth,
War was foundering of sblimities,
Extinction of each happy art and faith
By which the world had still kept head in air,
Protesting logic or protesting love,
Until the unendurable moment struck –
The inward scream, the duty to run mad.

And we recall the merry ways of guns –
Nibbling the walls of factory and church
Like a child, piecrust; felling groves of trees
Like a child, dandelions with a switch.
Machine-guns rattle toy-like from a hill,
Down in a row the brave tin-soldiers fall:
A sight to be recalled in elder days
When learnedly the future we devote
To yet more boastful visions of despair.

Julian Grenfell

Into Battle

The naked earth is warm with Spring,
   And with green grass and bursting trees
Leans to the sun's gaze glorying,
   And quivers in the sunny breeze;

And Life is Colour and Warmth and Light,
   And a striving evermore for these;
And he is dead who will not fight,
   And who dies fighting has increase.

The fighting man shall from the sun
   Take warmth, and life from the glowing earth;
Speed with the light-foot winds to run,
   And with the trees to ne'er birth;
And find, when fighting shall be done,
   Great rest, and fullness after dearth.
All the bright company of heaven
   Hold him in their high comradeship,
The Dog-Star and the Sisters Seven,
   Orion's Belt and sworded hip.

The woodland trees that stand together,
   They stand to him each one a friend;
They gently speak in the windy weather;
   They guide to valley and ridge's end.

The kestrel hovering by day,
   And the little owls that call by night,
Bid him be swift and keen as they,
   As keen of ear, as swift of sight.

The blackbird sings to him, 'Brother, brother,
   If this be the last song you shall sing,
Sing well, for you may not sing another;

Brother, sing.'

In dreary, doubtful, waiting hours,
  Before the brazen frenzy starts,
The horses show him nobler powers;
  O patient eyes, courageous hearts!

And when the burning moment breaks,
  And all things else are out of mind,
And only joy of battle takes
  Him by the throat, and makes him blind,

Through joy and blindness he shall know,
  Not caring much to know, that still
Nor lead nor steel shall reach him, so
  That it be not the Destined Will.

The thundering line of battle stands,
  And in the air Death moans and sings;
But Day shall clasp him with strong hands,
  And Night shall fold him in soft wings.

Thom Gunn

St. Martin and the Beggar

MARTIN sat young upon his bed
A budding cenobite,
Said 'Though I hold the principles
Of Christian life be right,
I cannot grow from them alone,
I must go out to fight.'

He travelled hard, he travelled far,
The light began to fail.
'Is not this act of mine,' he said,
'A cowardly betrayal,
should I not peg my nature down
with a religious nail?

Wind scudded on the marshland,
And, dangling at his side,
His sword soon clattered under hail:
What could he do but ride? –
There was not shelter for a dog,
The garrison far ahead.

A ship that moves on darkness
He rode across the plain,
When a brawny beggar started up
Who pulled at his rein
And leant dripping with sweat ands water
Upon the horse's mane.

He glared into Martin's eyes
With eyes more wild than bold;
His hair sent rivers down his spine;
Like a fowl packed to be sold
His flesh was grey. Martin said –
What, naked in this cold?

'I have no food to give you,
Money would be a joke.'
Pulling his new sword from the sheath
He took his soldier's cloak
And cut it in two equal parts
With a single stroke.

Grabbing one to his shoulders,
Pinning it with his chin,
The beggar dived into the dark,
And soaking to the skin
Martin went on slowly
Until he reached an inn.

On candle on the wooden table,
The food and drink were poor,
The woman hobbled off, he ate,
Then casually before
The table stood the beggar as
If he had used the door.

Now dry for hair and flesh had been
By warn airs fanned,
Still bare but round each muscled thigh
A single golden band,
His eyes now wild with love, he held,
The half cloak in his hand?

'You recognised the human need
Included yours, because
You did not hesitate, my saint,
To cut your cloak across;
But never since that moment
Did you regret the loss.

'My enemies would have turned away,
My holy toadies would
Have given all the cloak and frozen
Conscious that they were good.

But you, being a saint of men,
Gave only what you could.'

St. Martin stretched his hand out
To offer from his plate,
But the beggar vanished, thinking food
Like cloaks is needless weight.
Pondering on the matter,
St. Martin bent and ate.

Thomas Hardy

Afterwards

When the Present has latched its postern behind my tremulous stay,
    And the May month flaps its glad green leaves like wings,
Delicate-filmed as new-spun silk, will the neighbours say,
    'He was a man who used to notice such things'?

If it be in the dusk when, like an eyelid's soundless blink,
    The dewfall-hawk comes crossing the shades to alight
Upon the wind-warped upland thorn, a gazer may think,
    'To him this must have been a familiar sight.'

If I pass during some nocturnal blackness, mothy and warm,
    When the hedgehog travels furtively over the lawn,
One may say, 'He strove that such innocent creatures should come to
        no harm,
    But he could do little for them; and now he is gone.'

If, when hearing that I have been stilled at last, they stand at the
        door,
    Watching the full-starred heavens that winter sees,
Will this thought rise on those who will meet my face no more,
    'He was one who had an eye for such mysteries'?

And will any say when my bell of quittance is heard in the gloom,
    And a crossing breeze cuts a pause in its out-rollings,
Till they rise again, as they were a new bell's boom,
    'He hears it not now, but used to notice such things'?

Channel Firing

That night your great guns, unawares,
Shook all our coffins as we lay,
And broke the chancel window-squares,
We thought it was the Judgment-day

And sat upright. While drearisome
Arose the howl of wakened hounds:
The mouse let fall the altar-crumb,
The worms drew back into the mounds,

The glebe[3] cow drooled. Till God called, "No.
It's gunnery practice out at sea
Just as before you went below;
The world is as it used to be:

"All nations striving strong to make
Red war yet redder. Mad as hatters
They do no more for Christés sake
Than you who are helpless in such matters.

"That this is not the judgment-hour
For some of them's a blessed thing,
For it were they'd have to scour
Hell's floor for so much threatening. ...

"Ha, ha. It will be warmer when
I blow the trumpet (if indeed
I ever do; for you are men,
And rest eternal sorely need)."

Do down we lay again. "I wonder,
Will the world ever saner be,"
Said one, "than when He sent us under
In our indifferent century!"

And many a skeleton shook hi head.

---

[3] A small field

"Instead of preaching forty year,"
My neighbour Parson Thirdly said,
"I wish I had stuck to pies and beer."

Again the guns disturbed the hour,
Roaring their readiness to avenge,
As far inland as Stourton Tower,
And Camelot, and starlit Stonehenge.

Shut Out That Moon

Close up the casement, draw the blind,
    Shot out that stealing moon,
She wears too much the guise she wore
    Before our lutes were strewn
With years-deep dust, and names we read
    On a white stone were hewn.

Step not out on the dew-dashed lawn
    To view the Lady's Chair,
Immense Orion's glittering form,
    The Less and Greater Bear:
Stay in; to such sights we were drawn
    When faded ones were fair.

Brush not the bough for midnight scents
    That come forth lingeringly,
And wake the same sweet sentiments
    They breathed to you and me
When living seemed a laugh, and love
    All it was said to be.

Within the common lamp-it room
    Prison my eyes and thought;
Let dingy details crudely loom,
    Mechanic speech be wrought:
Too flagrant was Life's early bloom,
    Too tart the fruit it brought!

Work

THERE is no point in work
unless it absorbs you
like an absorbing game.

If it doesn't absorb you
if it's never any fun,
don't do it.

When a man goes out into his work
he is alive like a tree in spring
he is living, nor merely working.

When the Hindus weave thin wool into long, long lengths of stuff
with their thin dark hands and their wide dark eyes and their still
      souls absorbed
they are like slender trees putting forth leaves, a long white web of
      living leaf,
the tissue they weave,
and they clothe themselves in white as a tree clothes itself in its own
      foliage.

As with cloth, so with houses, ships, shoes, wagons or cups or
      loaves
men might put them forth as a snail its shell, as a bird that leans
its breast against its nest, to make it round,
as the turnip models its round root, as the bush makes flowers and
      gooseberries,
putting them forth, not manufacturing them,
and cities might be as once they were, bowers grown out from the
      busy bodies of people.

And so it will be again, men will smash the machines.

At last, for the sake of clothing himself in his own leaf-like cloth
tissued from his life,
and dwelling in his own bowery house, like a beaver's nibbled
      mansion

and drinking from cups that came off his fingers like flowers off
    their five-fold stem,
he will cancel the machines we have got.

Frances E. W. Harper (1825-1911)

The Slave Auction

The sale began – young girls were there,
    Defenceless in their wretchedness,
Whose stifled sobs of deep despair
    Revealed their anguish and distress.

And mother stood with streaming eyes,
    And saw their dearest children sold;
Unheeded rose their bitter cries,
    While tyrants bartered them for gold.

And woman, with her love and truth –
    For these in sable forms may dwell –
Gaz'd on the husband of her youth,
    With anguish none may paint or tell.

And men, whose sole crime was their hue,
    The impress of their Maker's hand,
And frail and shrinking children, too,
    Were gathered in that mournful band.

Ye who have laid your love to rest,
    And wept above their lifeless clay,
Know not the anguish of that breast,
    Whose lov'd are rudely torn away.

Ye may not know how desolate
    Are bosoms rudely forced to part,
And how a dull and heavy weight
    Will press the life-drops from the heart.

Bury Me in a Free Land

Make me a grave where'er you will,
In a lowly plain, or a lofty hill;
Make it among earth's humblest graves,
But not in a land where men are slaves.

I could not rest if around my grave
I heard the steps of a trembling slave;
His shadow above my silent tomb
Would make it a place of fearful gloom.

I could not rest if I heard the tread
Of a coffle gang to the shambles led,
And the mother's shriek of wild despair
Rise like a curse on the trembling air.

I could not sleep if I saw the lash
Drinking her blood at each fearful gash,
And I saw her babes torn from her breast,
Like trembling doves from their parent nest.

I'd shudder and start if I heard the bay
Of bloodhounds seizing their human prey,
And I heard the captive plead in vain
As they bound afresh his galling chain.

If I saw young girls from their mothers' arms
Bartered and sold for their youthful charms,
My eye would flash with a mournful flame,
My death-paled cheek grow red with shame.

I would sleep, dear friends, where bloated might
Can rob no man of his dearest right;
My rest shall be calm in any grave
Where none can call his brother a slave.

I ask no monument, proud and high,
To arrest the gaze of the passers-by;
All that my yearning spirit craves,

Is bury me not in a land of slaves.

H. Herrick

To Daffodils

FAIR daffodils, we weep to see
   You haste away so soon:
As yet the early-rising sun
   Has not attain'd his noon.
       Stay, stay
     Until the hasting day
      Has run
     But to the evensong;
And having pray'd together, we
     Will go with you along.

We have short time to stay, as you,
   We have as short a spring;
As quick a growth to meet decay,
   As you, or anything.
      We die
     As your hours do, and dry
      Away
     Like to the summer's rain;
Or as the pearls of morning's dew,
     Ne'er to be found again.

Gerard Manley Hopkins

God's Grandeur

The world is charged with the grandeur of God.
    It will flame out, like shining from shook foil;
    It gathers to a greatness, like the ooze of oil
Crushed. Why do men then now not reck his rod?
Generations have trod, have trod, have trod;
    And all is seared with trade; bleared, smeared with toil;
    And wears man's smudge and shares man's smell: the soil
Is bare now, nor can foot feel, being shod.

And for all this, nature is never spent;
    There lives the dearest freshness deep down things;
And though the last lights off the black West went
    Of, morning, at the brown brink eastward, springs –
Because the Holy Ghost over the bent
    World broods with warm breast and with ah! Bright wings.

Spring

Nothing is so beautiful as spring –
    When weeds, in wheels, shoot long and lovely and lush;
    Thrush's eggs look little low heavens, and thrush
Through the echoing timber does so rinse and wring
The ear, it strikes like lightnings to hear him sing;
    The glassy peartree leaves and blooms, they brush
    The descending blue; that blue is all in rush
With richness; the racing lambs too have fair their fling.

What is all this juice and all this joy?
    A strain of the earth's sweet being in the beginning
In Eden garden. – Have, get, before it cloy,

    Before it cloud, Christ, lord, and sour with sinning,
Innocent mind and Mayday in girl and boy,
    Most, O maid's child, thy choice and worthy the winning.

Langston Hughes (1902-1967)

The Negro Speaks Of Rivers

I've known rivers:
I've known rivers ancient as the world and older than the flow of
    human blood in human veins.

My soul has grown deep like the rivers.

I bathed in the Euphrates when dawns were young.
I built my hut near the Congo and it lulled me to sleep.
I looked upon the Nile and raised the pyramids above it.
I heard the singing of the Mississippi when Abe Lincoln went down
    to New Orleans, and I've seen its muddy bosom turn all golden
    in the sunset.

I've known rivers:
Ancient dusky rivers.

My soul has grown deep like the rivers.

Cultural Exchange

In the Quarter of the Negroes
Where the doors are doors of paper
Dust of dingy atoms
Blows a scratchy sound.
Amorphous jack-o'-lanterns caper
And the wind won't wait for midnight
For fun to blow doors down.

By the river and the railroad
With fluid far-off going
Boundaries bind unbinding
A whirl of whistles blowing.
No trains or steamboats going –
Yet Leontyne's unpacking.

In the Quarter of the Negroes
Where the doorknob lets in Lieder
More than German ever bore,
Her yesterday past grandpa –
Not of her own doing –
In a pot of collard greens
Is gently stewing.

Pushcarts fold and unfold
In a supermarket sea.
And we better find out, mama,
Where is the colored Laundromat
Since we moved up to Mount Vernon.

In the pot behind the paper doors
On the old iron stove what's cooking?
What's smelling, Leontyne?
Lieder, lovely Lieder
And a leaf of collard green.
Lovely Lieder, Leontyne.

You know, right at Christmas
They asked me if my blackness,

Would it rub off?
I said, *Ask you mama.*

Dreams and nightmares!
Nightmares, dreams, oh!
Dreaming that the Negroes
Of the South have taken over —
Voted all the Dixiecrats
Right out of power —
Come the COLORED HOUR:
Martin Luther King is Governor of Georgia,
Dr. Rufus Clement his Chief Adviser,
A. Philip Randolph the High Grand Worthy,
In white pillared mansions
Sitting on their wide verandas,
Wealthy Negroes have white servants,
White sharecroppers work the black plantations,
And colored children have white mammies:
        Mammy Faubus
        Mammy Eastland
        Mammy Wallace
Dear, dear darling old white mammies —
Sometimes even buried with our family.
        Dear Old
        Mammy Faubus!
Culture, they say, *is a two-way street:*
Hand me my mint julep, mammy.
        Hurry up!
        Make haste!

James Weldon Johnson (1871-1938)

O Black and Unknown Bards

O black and unknown bards of long ago,
How came your lips to touch the sacred fire?
How, in you darkness, did you come to know
The power and beauty of the minstrel's lyre?
Who first from midst his bonds lifted his eyes?
Who first from out the still watch, lone and long,
Feeling the ancient faith of prophets rise
Within his dark-kept soul, burst into song?

Heart of what slave poured out such melody
As "Steal away to Jesus"? On its strains
His spirit must have nightly floated free,
Though still about his hands he felt his chains.
Who heard great "Jordan roll"? Whose starward eye
That breathed that comforting, melodic sigh,
"Nobody knows de trouble I see"?

What merely living clod, what captive thing,
Could up toward God through all its darkness grope,
And find within its deadened heart to sing
These songs of sorrow, love and faith, and hope?
How did it catch that subtle undertone,
That note in music heard not with the ears?
How sound the elusive reed so seldom blown,
Which stirs the soul or melts the heart to tears.

Not that great German master in his dream
Of harmonies that thundered amongst the stars
At the creation, ever heard a theme
Nobler that "Go down, Moses." Mark its bars
How like a mighty trumpet-call they stir
The blood. Such are the notes that men have sung
Going to valorous deeds; such tones there were
That helped make history when Time was young.

There is a wide, wide wonder in it all,
That from degraded rest and servile toil
The fiery spirit of the seer should call
These simple children of the sun and soil.
O black slave singers, gone, forgot, unfamed,
You – you alone, of all the long, long line
Of those who've sung untaught, unknown, unnamed,
Have stretched out upward, seeking the divine.

You sang not deeds of heroes or of kings;
No chant of bloody war, no exulting paean
Of arms-won triumphs; but your humble strings
You touched in chord with music empyrean.
You sang far better than you knew; the songs
That for your listener's hungry hearts sufficed
Still live, - but more than this to you belongs:
You sang a race from wood and stone to Christ.

J. Keats

To Autumn

SEASON of mists and mellow fruitfulness!
   Close bosom-friend of the maturing sun;
Conspiring with him how to load and bless
   With fruit the vines that round the thatch-eaves run;
To bend with apples the moss'd cottage-trees,
   And fill all fruit with ripeness to the core;
     To swell the gourd, and plump the hazel shells
   With a sweet kernel; to set budding more,
And till more, later flowers for the bees,
Until they think warm days will never cease,
     For summer has o'er-brimm'd their clammy cells.

Who hath not seen thee oft amid thy store?
   Sometimes whoever seeks abroad may find
Thee sitting careless on a granary floor,
   Thy hair soft-lifted by the winnowing wind
Or on a hair-reap'd furrow sound asleep,
   Drowsed with the fume of poppies, while thy hook
     Spares the next swath and all its twinèd flowers;
   And sometimes like a gleaner thou dost keep
Steady thy laden head across a brook;
Or by a cider-press, with patient look,
     Thou watchest the last oozings hours by hours.

Where are the songs of Spring? Ay, where are they?
   Think not of them, thou hast thy music too, —
While barrèd clouds bloom the soft-dying day,
   And touch the stubble-plains with rosy hue;
Then in a wailful choir the small gnats mourn
   Among the river sallows, borne aloft
     Or sinking as the light wind lives or dies;
   And full-grown lambs loud bleat from hilly bourn;
Hedge-crickets sing; and now with treble soft
The redbreast whistles from a garden-croft;

And gathering swallows twitter in the skies.

D. H. Lawrence

Piano

Softly, in the dusk, a woman is singing to me;
Taking me back down the vista of years, till I see
A child sitting under the piano, in the boom of the tingling strings
And pressing the small, poised feet of a mother who smiles as she
sings.

In spite of myself, the insidious mastery of song
Betrays me back, till the heart of me weeps to belong
To the old Sunday evenings at home, with winter outside
And hymns in the cosy parlour, the tinkling piano our guide.

So now it is vain for the singer to burst into clamour
With the great black piano appassionato[4]. The glamour
Of childish days is upon me, my manhood is cast
Down in the flood or remembrance, I weep like a child for the past.

Played with passion

Louis Maneice

The Creditor

THE quietude of a soft wind
Will not rescind
My debts to God, but gentle-skinned
His finger probes. I lull myself
In quiet in diet in riot in dreams
Till God retire and the door shut.
But
Now I am left in the fire-blaze
The peacefulness of the fire-blaze
Will not erase
My debts to God for His mind strays
Over and under and all ways
All days and always.

John Manifold

Fife Tune

ONE morning in spring
We marched from Devizes
All shapes and all sizes
Like beads on a string,
But yet a swing
We trod the bluemetal
And full of high fettle
We started to sing.

She ran down the stair
A twelve-year-old darling
And laughing and calling
She tossed her bright hair;
Then silent to stare
At the men flowing past her—
There were all she could master
Adoring her there.

It's seldom I'll see
A sweeter or prettier;
I doubt we'll forget her
In two years or three,
And lucky he'll be
She takes for a lover
While we are far over
The treacherous sea.

Claude McKay (1890-1948)

The Tired Worker

O whisper, O my soul! The afternoon
Is waning into evening, whisper soft!
Peace, O my rebel heart! for soon the moon
From out its misty veil will swing aloft!
Be patient, weary body, soon the night
Will wrap thee gently in her sable sheet,
And with a leaden sigh thou wilt invite
To rest thy tired hands and aching feet.
The wretched day was theirs, the night is mine;
Come tender sleep, and fold me to thy breast.
But what steals out the gray clouds red like wine?
Of dawn! O dreaded dawn! O let me rest.
Weary my veins, my brain, my life! Have pity!
No! once again the harsh, the ugly city.

Tiger

The white man is a tiger at my throat,
Drinking my blood as my life ebbs away,
And muttering that his terrible striped coat
Is Freedom's and portends the Light of Day.
Oh white man, you may suck up all my blood
And throw my carcass into potter's field,
But never will I say with you that mud
Is bread for Negroes! Never will I yield.

Europe and Africa and Asia wait
The touted New Deal of the New World's hand!
New systems will be built on race and hate,
The Eagle and the Dollar will command.
Oh! Lord! My body, and my heart too, break —
The tiger in his strength his thirst must slake!

If We Must Die

If we must die, let it not be like hogs
Hunted and penned in an inglorious spot,
While round us bark the mad and hungry dogs,
Making their mock at our accursed lot.
If we must die, O let us nobly die,
So that our precious blood may not be shed
In vain; then even the monsters we defy
Shall be constrained to honor us though dead!
O kinsmen! we must meet the common foe!
Though far outnumbered let us show us brave,
And for their thousand blows deal one deathblow!
What though before us lies the open graves?
Like men we'll face the murderous, cowardly pack,
Pressed to the wall, dying, but fighting back!

George Meredith

From "The Woods of Westermain"

ENTER these enchanted woods,
　　You who dare.
Nothing harms beneath the leaves
More than waves a swimmer cleaves.
Toss your heart up with the lark,
Foot at peace with mouse and worm,
　　Fair you fare.
Only at a dread of dark
Quaver, and they quit their form:
Thousand eyeballs under hoods
　　Have you by the hair.
Enter these enchanted woods,
　　You who dare.
Here the snake across your path
Stretches in his golden bath:
Mossy-footed squirrels leap
Soft as winnowing plumes of sleep:
Yaffles on a chuckle skim
Low to laugh from branches dim:
Up the pine, where sits the star,
Rattles deep the moth-winged jar.
Each has business of his own;
But should you distrust a tone,
　　Then beware.
Shudder all the haunted roods,
All the eyeballs under hoods
　　Shroud you in their glare.
Enter these enchanted woods,
　　You who dare.

Dudley Randall (1914-2000)

Ballad of Birmingham

"Mother dear, may I go downtown
instead of out to play,
and march the streets of Birmingham
in a freedom march today?"

"No, baby, no, you may not go,
for the dogs are fierce and wild,
and clubs and hoses, guns and jails
ain't good for a little child."

"But, mother, I won't be alone.
Other children will go with me,
and march the streets of Birmingham
to make our country free."

"No, baby, no, you may not go,
for I fear those guns will fire.
But you may go to church instead,
and sing in the children's choir."

She has combed and brushed her nightdark hair,
and bathed rose petal sweet,
and drawn white gloves on her small brown hands,
and white shoes on her feet.

The mother smiled to know her child
was in the sacred place,
but that smile was the last smile
to come upon her face.

For when she heard the explosion,
her eyes grew wet and wild.
She raced through the streets of Birmingham
calling for her child.

She clawed through bits of glass and brick,
then lifted out a shoe.
"O, here's the shoe my baby wore,
but, baby, where are you?"

Siegfried Sassoon

The Rear-Guard

(Hindenburg Line, April 1917.)

Groping along the tunnel, step by step,
He winked his prying torch wit patching glare
From side to side, and sniffed the unwholesome air.

Tins, boxes, bottles, shapes too vague to know,
A mirror smashed, the mattress from a bed;
And he, exploring fifty feet below
The rosy gloom of battle overhead.

Tripping, he grabbed the wall; saw some one lie
Humped at his feet, half-hidden by a rug,
And stooped to give the sleeper's arm a tug.
"I'm looking for headquarters." No reply.
"God blast your neck!" (For days he'd had no sleep.)

"Get up and guide me through this stinking place."
Savage, he kicked a soft, unanswering heap,
And flashed his beam across the livid face
Terribly glaring up, whose eyes yet wore
Agony dying hard ten days before;
And fists of fingers clutched a blackening wound.

Alone he staggered on until he found
Dawn's ghost that filtered down a shafted stair
To the dazed, muttering creatures underground
Who hear the boom of shells in muffled sound.
At last, with sweat of horror in his hair,
He climbed through darkness to the twilight air,
Unloading hell behind him step by step.

Dreamers

Soldiers are citizens of death's grey land,
    Drawing no dividend from time's to-morrows.
In the great hour to destiny they stand,
    Each with his feuds, and jealousies, and sorrows.

Soldiers are sworn to action; they must win
    Some flaming, fatal climax with their lives.
Soldiers are dreamers; when the guns begin
    They think of firelit homes, clean beds, and wives.

I see them in foul dug-outs, gnawed by rats,
    And in the ruined trenches, lashed with rain,
Dreaming of things they did with balls and bats,
    And mocked by hopeless longing to regain
Bank-holidays, and picture shows, and spats,
    And going to the office in the train.

SIR C. Spring-Rice

I Vow To Thee, My Country

I VOW to thee, my country – all earthly things above –
Entire and whole and perfect, the service of my love,
The love that asks no questions: the love that stands the test,
That lays upon the altar the dearest and the best:
The love that never falters, the love that pays the price,
The love that makes undaunted the final sacrifice.

And there's another country I've heard of long ago –
Most dear to them that love her, most great to them that know –
We may not count her armies: we may not see her King –
Her fortress is a faithful heart, her pride is suffering –
And soul by soul and silently her shinning bounds increase.
And her ways are ways of gentleness and all her paths are peace.

Lord Tennyson

Crossing The Bar

SUNSET and evening star,
  And one clear call for me!
And may there be no moaning of the bar,
  When I put out to sea,

But such a tide as moving seems asleep,
  Too full for sound and foam,
When that which drew from out the boundless deep
  Turns again home.

Twilight and evening bell,
  And after that the dark!
And may there be no sadness of farewell,
  When I embark;

For tho' from out our bourne of Time and Place
  The flood may bear me far,
I hope to see my Pilot face to face
  When I have crost the bar.

Edward Thomas

The Owl

Downhill I came, hungry, and yet not starved;
Cold, yet had heat within me that was proof
Against the North wind; tired, yet so that rest
Had seemed the sweetest thing under a roof.

Then at the inn I had food, fire, and rest,
Knowing how hungry, cold, and tired was I.
All of the night was quite barred out except
An owl's cry, a most melancholy cry

Shaken out long and clear upon the hill,
No merry note, nor cause of merriment,
But one telling me plain what I escaped
And other could not, that night, as in I went.

And salted was my food, and my repose,
Salted and sobered, too, by the bird's voice
Speaking for all who lay under the stars,
Soldiers and poor, unable to rejoice.

Oscar Wilde

The Harlot's House

We caught the tread of dancing feet,
We loitered down the moonlit street,
And stopped beneath the harlot's house.

Inside, above the din and fray,
We heard the loud musicians play
The "Treues Liebes Herz" of Strauss.[5]

Like strange mechanical grotesques,
Making fantastic arabesques,
The shadows raced across the blind.

We watched the ghostly dancers spin
To sound of horn and violin,
Like black leaves wheeling in the wind.

Like wire-pulled automatons,
Slim silhouetted skeletons
Went sidling through the slow quadrille.

They took each other by the hand,
And danced a stately saraband;
Their laughter echoed thin and shrill.

Sometimes a clockwork puppet pressed
A phantom lover to her breast,
Sometimes they seemed to try to sing.

Sometimes a horrible marionette
Came out, and smoke its cigarette
Upon the steps like a live thing.

"Heart of True Love," a waltz by the Austrian composer Johann Strauss (1825-
899).

Then, turning to my love, I said,
"The dead are dancing with the dead,
The dust is whirling with the dust."

But she – she heard the violin,
And left my side, and entered in:
Love passed into the house of lust.

The suddenly the tune went false,
The dancers wearied of the waltz,
The shadows ceased to wheel and whirl.

And down the long and silent street,
The dawn, with silver-sandalled feet,
Crept like a frightened girl.

Walt Whitman

To A Locomotive in Winter

Thee for my recitative,
Thee in the driving storm even as now, the snow the winter-day
    declining,
Thee in thy panoply, thy measur'd dual throbbing and thy beat
    convulsive,
Thy back cylindric body, golden brass and silvery steel,
Thy ponderous side-bars, parallel and connecting rods, gyrating,
    shuttling at thy sides,
Thy metrical, now swelling pant and roar, now tapering in the
    distance,
Thy great protruding head-light fix'd in front,
Thy long, pale, floating vapour-pennants, tangent with delicate
    purple,
The dense and murky clouds out-belching from thy smoke-stack,
Thy knitted frame, thy springs and valves, the tremulous twinkle of
    the wheels,
Thy train of cars behind, obedient, merrily following,
Through gale or calm, now swift, now slack, yet steadily careering;
Type of the modern – emblem of motion and power – pulse of the
    continent,
For once come serve the Muse and merge in verse, even as here I see
    thee,
With storm and buffering gusts of wind and falling snow,
By day thy warning ringing bell to sound its notes,
By night thy silent signal lamps to swing.

Fierce-throated beauty!
Roll through my chant with all thy lawless music, thy swinging lamps
    at night,
Thy madly-whistled laughter, echoing, rumbling like an earthquake,
    rousing all,
Law of thyself complete, thine own track firmly holding,
No sweetness debonair of tearful harp or glib piano thine,)
Thy trills of shrieks by rocks and hills return'd,

Launch'd o'er the prairies wide, across the lakes,
To the free skies unpent and glad and strong.

William Wordsworth (1770-1827)

It Is A Beauteous Evening

It is a beauteous evening, calm and free,
The holy time is quiet as a Nun
Breathless with adoration; the broad sun
Is sinking down in its tranquility;
The gentleness of heaven broods o'er the Sea:
Listen! The mighty Being is awake,
And doth with his eternal motion make
A sound like thunder – everlastingly.
Dear Child! Dear Girl! That walkest with me here,
If thou appear untouched by solemn thought,
Thy nature is not therefore less divine:
Thou liest in Abraham's bosom all the year;
And worshippest at the Temple's inner shrine,
God being with thee when we know it not.

I Wandered Lonely As a Cloud

I wandered lonely as a cloud
That floats on high o'er vales and hills,
When all at once I saw a crowd,
A host, of golden daffodils;
Beside the lake, beneath the trees,
Fluttering and dancing in the breeze.

Continuous as the stars that shine
And twinkle on the milky way,
They stretched in never-ending line
Along the margin of a bay:
Ten thousand saw I at a glance,
Tossing their heads in sprightly dance.

The waves beside them danced; but they
Outdid the sparkling waves in glee;

A poet could not but be gay,
In such a jocund company;
I gazed – and gazed – but little thought
What wealth the show to me had brought:

For oft, when on my couch I lie
In vacant or in pensive mood,
They flash upon that inward eye
Which is the bliss of solitude;
And then my heart with pleasure fills,
And dances with the daffodils.

William Butler Yeats

On The Subjugation Of Switzerland

TWO voices are there; one is of the sea,
One of the mountains; each a mighty voice;
In both from age to age thou dist rejoice;
They were thy chosen music, Liberty.
There came a tyrant, and with holy glee
Thou fought'st against him; but hast vainly striven:
Thou from thy Alpine holds at length art driven,
Where not a torrent murmurs heard by thee.
Of one deep bliss thine ear hath been bereft;
Then cleave, O cleave to that which still is left;
For, high-souled maid, what sorrow would it be
That mountain floods should thunder as before,
And ocean bellow from his rocky shore,
And neither awful voice be heard by thee!

The Second Coming

Turning and turning in the widening gyre
The falcon cannot hear the falconer;
Things fall apart; the centre cannot hold;
Mere anarchy is loosed upon the world,
The blood-dimmed tide is loosed, and everywhere
The ceremony of innocence is drowned;
The best lack all conviction, while the worst
Are full of passionate intensity.

Surely some revelation is at hand;
Surely the Second Coming is at hand.
The Second Coming! Hardly are those words out
When a vast image out of *Spiritus Mundi*
Troubles my sight: somewhere in sands of the desert
A shape with lion body and the head of a man,
A gaze blank and pitiless as the sun,

Is moving its slow thighs, while all about it
Reel shadows of the indignant desert birds.
The darkness drops again; but now I know
That twenty centuries of stony sleep
Were vexed to nightmare by a rocking cradle
And what rough beast, its hour come round at last,
Slouches toward Bethlehem to be born?

No Second Troy

Why should I blame her that she filled my days
With misery, or that she would of late
Have taught to ignorant men most violent ways,
Or hurled the little streets upon the great,
Had they but courage equal to desire?
What could have made her peaceful with a mind
That nobleness made simple as a fire,
With beauty like a tightened bow, a kind
That is not natural in an age like this,
Being high and solitary and most stern?
Why, what could she have done, being what she is?
Was there another Troy for her to burn?

The Magi

Now as at all times I can see in the mind's eye,
In their stiff, painted clothes, pale unsatisfied ones
Appear and disappear in the blue depth of the sky
With all their ancient faces like rain-beaten stones,
And all their helms of silver hovering side by side,
And all their eyes still fixed, hoping to find once more,
Being by Calvary's turbulence unsatisfied,
The uncontrollable mystery on the bestial floor.